No Longer Welcome

No Longer Welcome

The Epidemic of Expulsion from Early Childhood Education

KATHERINE M. ZINSSER

OXFORD
UNIVERSITY PRESS

OXFORD
UNIVERSITY PRESS

Oxford University Press is a department of the University of Oxford. It furthers the University's objective of excellence in research, scholarship, and education by publishing worldwide. Oxford is a registered trade mark of Oxford University Press in the UK and certain other countries.

Published in the United States of America by Oxford University Press
198 Madison Avenue, New York, NY 10016, United States of America.

CIP data is on file at the Library of Congress

ISBN 978–0–19–763971–9

DOI: 10.1093/med-psych/9780197639719.001.0001

1 3 5 7 9 8 6 4 2

Printed by Integrated Books International, United States of America

For Graeson and Ashleigh

Contents

1
Introduction

Lance is a curious, energetic little boy who lives in southern Illinois with his Dad, Stephen, and his stepmom. As a toddler, Lance took easily to art and loved animals. When I interviewed Stephen in 2020, Lance was about halfway through his kindergarten year at the local public school and was thriving, but it had been a long and frustrating road to get there. Between the ages of 2 and 5, Lance attended and was expelled from, or pushed out of, seven different child-care programs.

The first and most formal expulsion came on the heels of his parents' messy separation, "Things were tense. We disagreed about many things, including child-care arrangements," Stephen explained. As tensions grew at home, incident reports started coming home with Lance. The 2-year-old was biting and being bitten more frequently and was struggling to manage his emotions and behaviors. Then one weekend, a letter arrived informing his parents that Lance was no longer enrolled at the child-care center, effective immediately.

Although not as formally documented, Stephen considers the second exclusion another expulsion, "They asked us to withdraw him." Lance had only been at the next program, a home-based child-care program, for a few weeks before he started hitting and biting other children. At the next program, the provider quipped at pick up, "You need to do something about him," before asking them to find another placement. It was clear that she was not willing or able to handle having Lance in her home.

Lance was doing "pretty well" at the Catholic church preschool Stephen found near his home until the director happened to mention in passing one day that Lance had to eat by himself in a separate room "because he gets handsy around other kids." Stephen was appalled. Rather than trying to help his son learn how to be a part of a community, they relegated him to a closet to eat in isolation while other children enjoyed a family-style meal. "They were not teaching him. They were punishing him for being a hungry, eager 2-year-old." Stephen took Lance home that evening and never brought him back. He felt like he had no choice but to withdraw his son.

At the YMCA, Stephen tried a different tact—he was upfront and honest. "I told them he had had some issues with aggression in the past," but the director led him to believe that they were prepared to work with Lance. Less than 2 weeks later, though, the phone call came—Lance was expelled for being too aggressive. Stephen had long exhausted the meager local child-care options and several in the neighboring county where his ex-wife lived. "I felt like we were running out of options . . . things were getting desperate because we needed full-time care so that I could get to work."

Desperation led Stephen to enroll Lance at StarKids (pseudonym), a program that already had a bad reputation on Yelp. His fears were confirmed when a few weeks later, Stephen was called in to pick Lance up early because he was misbehaving. When Stephen arrived, the director looked at the little boy and said, "You're being bad. We don't want you here, so your dad is going to take you home." Stephen was shocked and scared for his son. "Even now, more than a year later, when we drive by that program, Lance remembers it as a place he was not wanted."

Stephen had great sympathy for the staff at the next program Lance attended. It was "disgusting and run down . . . the staff was paid minimum wage, they were young, inexperienced and exhausted." Maybe, he surmised, the high demand for care in the region meant that programs could continue operating despite poor conditions and inadequate staffing. He did not see the director of this program as malicious, just overwhelmed, and unable to cope with children who did not conform to their strict expectations. "He wasn't expelled exactly; the director just said he wasn't welcome to return until he was medicated."

Fed up with this revolving door and distressed by the impact the lack of consistency and constant negativity was having on his son, Stephen started calling the school district. Although he had always known that the district offered a prekindergarten program, Stephan had never considered it because it was part-time. Nevertheless, at this point, he was missing so much work because of the constant search for child care and coming to pick Lance up early when programs suspended him. Stephen figured part-time was better than nothing at all. Lance was placed on a waitlist, but Stephen persisted, calling the superintendent's office regularly and pleading his case. Lance's story was moving, and soon he was bumped to the front of the line.

"He's really thrived. His speech has exploded!" Stephen said, "the teachers love him. They describe him as empathic and a good friend. I finally feel like someone is seeing the same boy I see at home." Reflecting on this terrible cycle, Stephen suspects that Lance's aggression had been reinforced, "He learned, 'if I'm bad, I get

to go home and be with Dad!' " Now that the public program is accommodating him so well, Lance is not desperate to leave. Lance was formally diagnosed with attention deficit disorder in the summer before kindergarten, and instead of forcing Stephen to pursue medication, the school adjusted the classroom ratios, bringing in a behavioral aide as needed, and establishing an Individualized Education Program (IEP) for Lance. Stephen also eagerly shared that "the teachers filled out the right forms, and now insurance will cover some additional supports, like group therapy, something I wish we had had for our older son."

***

Lance's story is heart-wrenching but illustrative. Every exclusion took a significant toll on the family and tainted their transition into kindergarten. Stephen missed substantial amounts of work picking Lance up early or staying home with him while they searched for new care arrangements. Even while at work, Stephen reported feeling distracted—worried about how Lance was being treated at school, or making contingency plans in case he was expelled again. Financially, the family lost deposits and tuition payments as program's contracts specified that refunds would not be given in the case of problematic behavior or voluntary dis-enrollment. More distressing for Stephen, though, was seeing how these experiences soured his and his son's enjoyment and enthusiasm about school. Understandably, Stephen reported that it took a long time for him to trust the school district and Lance's new teachers at the public school. Even though he should have been able to take a deep breath knowing that his son was relatively safe from another immediate expulsion, Stephen felt on edge for a long time. Lance, too, took a while to warm up to new teachers and routines. Toward the end of our interview, Stephen quipped, "We both finally came around, but it could have gone either way."

Likely, one of the most critical reasons that Lance is thriving now is because of Stephen. He had become a fierce advocate on the issue of early childhood expulsion, lobbying in the state capital, Springfield, for the passage of legislation to prohibit the use of expulsion in early childhood programs, raising alarms about the inadequate pay and support of the child-care workforce, and organizing other parents on social media who have been through similar plights. Lance's story is not yet complete, and Stephen still feels like he needs to be vigilant: "you hear a lot of stories about kids who have been expelled getting into serious trouble."

The stories Stephen is referencing have also been well documented in the research literature. We have amassed decades worth of research showing that children who experienced exclusionary discipline like expulsion and suspension from K–12 schools are more likely to come into contact with the juvenile justice system and be incarcerated as adults. There is no parallel body of literature on the long-term consequences of exclusion from early childhood education programs, but as Lance's story shows, we can expect the impacts to be significant and to affect not just the child but their families and communities. One trend that is well depicted in Lance's story and the research literature is that children who have been excluded are also at higher risk for future exclusions (Hwang, 2018). The earlier this pattern is established, the more likely children are to be expelled in elementary school, resulting in greater losses in cumulative instructional time and more significant achievement gaps separating removed children from their included peers, particularly during critical periods of development. As we see in Lance's story, children who are expelled for misbehavior or noncompliance are most often the ones in need of the enhanced social and emotional support and learning that is foundational to early childhood education.

The Ecology of Expulsion

Although the individual child may be at the center of any discussion of early childhood exclusionary discipline, the settings and the people with whom the child comes into contact determine the child's fate. We can envision children as developing at the center of a set of concentric rings of influence. Although each child possesses unique biological characteristics and temperamental traits, their developmental trajectory is intimately guided by interactions with their families, peers, teachers, communities, and culture—components that themselves interact and shift over time. This bio-ecological model of human development (Bronfenbrenner & Morris, 2006) has been used to describe and explain a wide array of developmental processes, and is similarly at the center of the expulsion and exclusion process. An adult makes the decision to expel, but the context influences that adult.

Early childhood education programs are complex ecologies with many internal and external forces and factors influencing the lives of all involved. Within a classroom, resources, physical space and structures, and relationships among and between children and teachers interact with teachers' training and background. These dynamic interactions shift over time as the actors become more familiar with each other, and children grow and learn. At the same time, factors outside of the classroom door, such as parents' relationships with the school and teachers, how the administrators and workplaces support and compensate the teachers, and policies and funding requirements that regulate interactions and resources, as well as individual and societal prejudices and biases, all work together to influence teachers' perceptions of and responses to children's behavior.

The interconnectedness of these layers—children, parents, teachers, programs, communities, and policy—can be a powerful force for good. Dollars invested in providing high-quality child care and enrichment to young children early in life pay dividends for generations to come, not just by boosting individual children's school readiness, but also by supporting parents' return to the workforce, employing community members, and reducing expenditures on social safety-net programs and the criminal justice system. Longitudinal studies continue to find robust lifelong effects of high-quality early childhood education. The Perry Preschool Project (Schweinhart, 1993), the Abecedarian Project (Campbell et al., 2002), and the Chicago School Readiness Project (Watts et al., 2018) have all shown early childhood education to be a potent and pervasive intervention that even has multi-generational benefits that transfer beyond the individual. For example, in the most recent analysis of the Perry Preschool study data, Nobel laureate James Heckman and colleagues (Heckman et al., 2010; Heckman & Karapakula, 2019) found that children of the grown participants of the early childhood program are less likely to have been suspended from school, and more likely to graduate from high school. Random assignment into the Perry program decades prior resulted in participants developing stronger families of their own, and significantly contributed to the next generation's upward mobility.

Although many have touted the power of early childhood education as a force for good, the interconnected system also leaves children vulnerable to the whims of adults—both close to them and very distant. As was drawn into sharp contrast by the COVID-19 pandemic, our nation's early care and education system is fragile—precariously balanced on the backs of working families and reliant on political desire. As in natural ecologies, where pollution or blight in one area can have ripple effects throughout, we can conceptualize each child's expulsion as an outcome of a more pervasive malady—an overburdened, underfunded, undervalued, and fragmented early education system.

The intricate relationships among people, structures, and policies in early childhood education make unpacking and understanding why and how expulsion happens rather tricky, and identifying solutions that work well across a variety of delivery systems nearly impossible. This book cannot and will not accomplish these tasks satisfactorily. However, I believe that it can be a first step toward moving the conversation on the early childhood expulsion crisis out into the broader community. Those in the field have known for over a decade that expulsion in early childhood is happening at staggering rates—more than three times that of K–12 school children—and while there has been much handwringing and wishing it away, there has also been substantial progress toward identifying plausible interventions. The implications of early expulsion reach well beyond those who work with and on behalf of young children and families. Just as the benefit of investments in early childhood pay dividends for communities, so too can breakdowns in the system prove costly. Children's experiences in early childhood education accumulate and travel with them for the rest of their lives. Our failure to properly support and retain children in early learning settings will result in more considerable strain on K–12 school systems to address children's social, emotional, and behavioral needs.

When friends and colleagues learn that I study preschool expulsion, their first reaction is always disbelief. Yes, I have to tell them, it does really happen, to thousands of children each year. They often then express some level of collective remorse ("What is wrong with our country?") because they know that being expelled can have long-term negative consequences. Although research into the exact consequences of early childhood expulsion is minimal, we know from the study of older children that implications can be academically and psychologically severe and touch the lives of families and communities at large. Before we spend the remainder of this book trying to understand how, and why, and from where early childhood expulsions occur, we need to pause and remember what is at stake. When we exclude thousands of young children each year, what are the real costs to them, their family, and our society at large?

Academic Consequences

By definition, exclusion from school means removing a child from a structured learning environment and thereby decreasing their opportunities to keep up academically. A recent meta-analysis synthesizing over 30 studies of suspension between 1986 and 2012 (Noltemeyer et al., 2015) demonstrated that even temporary removals from school (fewer than 10 days) had significant negative impacts on students' achievement test scores. Children who are pushed out of the classroom for disciplinary reasons cannot and do not perform as well on measures of academic learning. Over time, iterative exclusions have compounding effects, not just because of time spent out of the classroom, but also because excluded children lose additional time trying to catch up with course material. Exclusionary discipline, therefore, fuels the widening of achievement gaps, particularly during critical periods of development, like early childhood (Arcia, 2006; Christle et al., 2007; Lee et al., 2011). Studies have also pointed to a cumulative school-wide effect of lost learning time too. Schools with higher suspension rates have lower mean scores on state achievement tests than schools that utilize suspension less frequently as a form of discipline (Skiba & Rausch, 2004).

When a classmate (or several classmates) are leaving and re-entering the classroom sporadically over the year, it can take a toll on collective progress through the curriculum. Teachers and classmates may expend time helping a student catch up, or instructional time may be lost, differentiating instruction for the student(s) who are behind. However, the narrow focus on core academic subjects and achievement tests will not tell the full story of the consequences of school exclusion, because not all learning, especially in early childhood, is captured by these standardized assessments.

Loss of Affinity

Not every child is explicitly told they are not wanted, as Lance regrettably was. Nevertheless, excluded children routinely report feeling alienated from school and feeling less and less affinity for a specific school and for schooling in general. Unsurprisingly, this alienation makes them more likely to drop out altogether (Archambault et al., 2009). Children who have experienced repeated exclusions are accustomed to being thought of as "bad kids"—teachers and administrators may overtly label them as such or may treat them differently, as we saw in the case of Lance eating in isolation. Likewise, other children in the classroom observe the way one or a small set of children are repeatedly excluded, sent home early, or admonished, thereby learning who belongs or is welcome in their school, and who is not, perpetuating an exclusionary school climate (Ispa-Landa, 2018; Lewis & Diamond, 2015). It is easy to see how a child would not enjoy being around people who perceive them as bad or out of place. Even more concerning, students report that when teachers and peers scorn them over time, they begin to view themselves as being a threat or danger to others (Welch & Payne, 2010). This negative feedback loop results in an uptick in unwanted behaviors as children who are suspended or expelled react poorly to feeling unwelcome at school. Moreover, just as children who miss out on learning time struggle to catch up with their peers academically, children excluded from social-learning opportunities in the classroom cannot make up for that learning while isolated at home.

This loss of social-emotional learning time is particularly costly in early childhood, a critical period for the development of skills related to emotion recognition and regulation, and forming and maintaining relationships. When children struggle with letter recognition or mimicking phonic sounds, we have numerous curricula, interventions, supports, and specialists ready to intervene and provide extra help. When a child struggles to manage their emotions, control their behaviors, or interact positively with peers and adults, however, time and time again, they are excluded from the very context and resources they will need to learn more pro-social skills. You cannot learn social skills while eating lunch in an empty closet or sitting in the director's office waiting for your parent to pick you up early.

Lifelong Implications

In addition to these more proximal academic and social-emotional costs, researchers have traced significant lifelong adverse outcomes to school exclusion, most notably, delinquency and incarceration. For older children, removal from school most likely results in them spending more time unsupervised or poorly supervised, socializing with other out-of-school youth, and in contexts ripe for delinquent behavior that could lead to an arrest. Prior studies have shown that higher levels of parental involvement and monitoring are associated with lower levels of adolescent delinquency (Lahey et al., 2008). Children who were repeatedly suspended were eight times more likely to be incarcerated than those never suspended (Losen, 2015). Students who have been suspended or expelled are more likely to drop out which places them at risk of experiencing financial insecurity and relying on public economic assistance (Waldfogel et al., 2007). Further, correlational studies have shown associations between school exclusion and later substance use problems (Townsend et al., 2007). Although many of these frightening outcomes may feel far removed from the preschool classroom, early experiences of exclusion can trigger a cascade of negative interactions with schools.

Ripple Effects of Early Exclusion

In line with our broader ecological thinking about children and families, it is essential that we also consider the impact of exclusions from care not just on the child, but on the family unit. There have been very few studies of the direct effects of young children's exclusions on parents and family units, and none, to date, has followed children over time. In a 2014 qualitative dissertation study with a small sample of parents whose children had been recently expelled or pushed out of preschools, Tasha Henneman of Mills College (2014) identified several effects of the exclusion on their families. Parents reported temporary employment issues, such as having to leave work suddenly to retrieve a child, and lost hours and wages; two parents quit altogether when they could not find alternative care. For many families, losing a job also means losing eligibility for a child-care subsidy, making the search for alternative care even more difficult, if not impossible, to afford. The catch-22 of not being able to work because your child is not in care and not being able to afford care because you are not working weighs heavily on many families, regardless of whether or not they have been excluded. In a replication of the K–12 findings, Henneman's families reported that the excluded children had internalized that they were "bad boys." As one parent was quoted (2014, p. 77), "It has been messing with his self-esteem, and after a while he is like, ok, 'I am just stupid, I am mad at myself. I am never good. I don't do anything good.'" It is hard to see a 4-year-old internalize these negative messages. The constant parroting of negativity took a toll on the parents. Their sense of self-efficacy and perceptions of themselves as "good parents" were further eroded when several were criticized and blamed by family and friends for their child's expulsion.

The emotional impact of a child's exclusion on the parents has been documented in studies with older children as well. In a separate qualitative study, parents whose children had been suspended reported a range of emotional reactions from anger to shock to embarrassment. To some extent, the child's exclusion was a reflection of them or their parenting. The study authors, Gibson and Haight (2013), also noted that parents used plural pronouns when describing the disciplinary action. For example, parents were quoted as saying, "When they suspended *us*..." (p. 269), indicating that parents felt a shared identity with the disciplined child.

There is no doubt that we need additional research into family-level short- and long-term consequences of exclusionary discipline at all ages. However, even based on the limited literature available, it is clear that attention needs to be paid to both proximal and more distal negative consequences—especially the financial and psychological implications for whole family units. Nevertheless, we would be remiss to assume that these negative consequences are evenly distributed across all children in our country. Like many other social processes in our nation, school discipline is enacted unequally across gender and racial lines. There is no exception for younger children in child care. Thousands of children, especially boys and Black[1] children, are being expelled from child-care and preschool programs each year. But to point at children's identities as "risk factors" denies the ways that the contexts in which children live and learn are the perpetrators of risk: places where adults perceive some children—even 2- and 3-year-old children—as problematic, or even dangerous, primarily because of the color of their skin.

This book seeks to describe better the contexts within which these harsh disciplinary decisions are being made and to consider the multitude of factors—from dyadic relationships to state-level policy—that can mitigate or exacerbate our nation's child-care systems' reliance on exclusionary discipline. We begin in Chapter 2 by defining what constitutes early childhood exclusion and the scope of the problem—the sheer number of and disparities in children being excluded. In Chapter 3, we examine the explanation provided for these exclusions: challenging behaviors. Beyond describing examples of the types of behaviors that precede teachers' and programs' decisions to expel a child, we will review the research literature on the impacts of early adversity and trauma on children's social and emotional development. Chapter 4, however, challenges us to consider how our interpretation of children's behavior is in itself subjective and heavily influenced by implicit bias. Through experimental studies and recent headlines, we will connect teachers' unconscious

[1] Throughout this text, I use the term "Black" to refer to individuals of African ancestry regardless of the terminology used in the original studies cited. Nomenclature and identity designations have varied over time, and this choice is in line with the current style manual of the American Psychological Association and respects individuals' varied cultural backgrounds and family histories.

biases to perceptions of and reactions to children's behavior across racial and gender lines. Chapter 5 considers the contexts in which teachers are making disciplinary decisions, shining a light on the effects of stress, poor working conditions, and insufficient resources. With this background, we then examine in Chapter 6 the actual processes of excluding a child and program-level differences in policies—from interactions with families to utilization of interventions—that may alter the risk of expulsion. Expulsions also occur within the context of relationships, and Chapter 7 describes research into the importance of and support for positive parent-teacher relationships. In Chapters 8 and 9, we will investigate promising paths forward through changes in practice and policy, including emerging results of a multi-year collaborative evaluation of a progressive legislative effort to end early childhood expulsion here in Illinois. Chapter 10 emphasizes how our ability to understand and address exclusionary discipline is dependent reliable data. This book ends with a galvanizing call to action, written by Dr. Iheoma Iruka, an expert in racial equity and early childhood education policy.

I have come to write this book from a place of deep and broad empathy—for the children and families, of course, but first for the teachers. My research into preschool expulsion emerged out of over a decade of work on teachers' mental health and workplace well-being. As the daughter of a former nursery school administrator, I grew up seeing behind the curtains of running a preschool program—the intense demands on teachers, the exhaustion and burnout, and the tension with families and colleagues. My research training on children's social-emotional development helped open doors to think through the multiple layers of influence affecting children's and teachers' emotions at school. With a fellowship from the National Academy of Education early in my career, I was able to pivot and specifically begin examining how structural, inter-, and intra-personal factors guide teachers' and administrators' disciplinary decisions in early childhood.

The reader should be forewarned, however, that this book will not offer satisfactory solutions to this crisis. Despite 15 years of evidence of its occurrence, broad consensus that it is harmful, and a myriad of policy efforts against it, the expulsion of young children continues unchecked. This book will touch on promising policies, practices, and interventions that may help, but the main goal of this book is to keep the conversation front and center and keep us from collectively wiping our hands of the crisis.

Throughout this book, I weave together the results of my own research, stories from dozens of interviews with teachers, parents, and stakeholders, and evidence from the growing existing literature. I use stories throughout to illustrate the complexity and humanity of this crisis. In order to protect individuals' identities, I have made small changes to the details of these stories, but for the most part, they represent what families and providers shared directly with me during interviews.

While I have amassed a great deal of knowledge and experience on the subject of early childhood exclusion, my identities as a White mother and developmental psychologist necessarily influence my perception and presentation of this research. My identity also shaped my research agenda. Moving to Chicago, a city with a legacy of segregation and disproportionate opportunities, and taking a position in a community psychology program helped me confront the early and oppressive racism in our education system. At the University of Illinois at Chicago, I felt empowered to leverage my scientific training to seek out opportunities for intervention. This positionality has influenced the questions I ask, the community partnerships I build, the ways I make sense of available resources, and the solutions I advance in this text and elsewhere. At the same time, I am not expert in every topic raised here, and I strongly recommend that readers supplement this text by reading the works of others from a wide range of backgrounds to gain additional perspectives and depth of understanding.

2
Defining the Problem

The U.S. Department of Education (DOE)'s Office of Civil Rights began collecting data on discipline rates in the 1960s, primarily to ascertain whether children of color were receiving equivalent educational experiences following school integration. It will come as no surprise that ever since those original surveys of student demographics, there have been stark, persistent disparities reported. These annual reports issued by the DOE provide clear, reliable data sets to researchers studying the use of exclusionary discipline in our nation's public schools. However, there is no equivalent data set for our early childhood sector. We have no way to systematically gather data on or from programs serving children between the ages of birth and 5 years old, be they in community-based child care, publicly funded preschools, or home care. The DOE did not even collect data on preschool-age children in classrooms located within public schools until the 2011–2012 school year. Even when the annual civil rights data collection was expanded to include prekindergarten students, it still omits the majority of early childhood programs. Outside the purview of the DOE are any community-based child-care or preschool programs that are not regulated by the state boards of education, including Head Start programs.

This lack of coordinated data systems can go a long way toward explaining why we know so little about the prevalence of early childhood exclusionary discipline. To fill this void and understand whether, how, and from where children are excluded, we must look to a hodge-podge of state and research reports, each of which has devised slightly different ways of gathering data.

One of the first surveys of early childhood exclusionary practices was mailed to nearly 500 preschool and child-care administrators in Detroit in 1999. The Michigan State agency distributing the survey was attempting to ascertain the extent to which child-care programs needed access to early childhood mental health consultation services. Although only about a quarter of the administrators responded, the data were unsettling. Administrators reported that for every 1,000 children enrolled, they expelled 27.5 children because they felt they could not manage their behavior. The pervasive use of expulsion and exclusion was soon replicated across several other studies using a wide array of samples.

In 2002, researchers at the University of Illinois at Chicago and the Erikson Institute included questions about exclusionary discipline in a more extensive study of infant and toddler program mental health needs. Over 600 programs providing prevention, early intervention, public health, and child-care services to infants and toddlers were surveyed across Illinois. Among many results related to the substantial need for increased access to resources and services, this report indicated that 40% of child-care programs had had to ask a child under the age of 3 to leave the program because of social, emotional, or behavioral problems (Cutler & Gilkerson, 2002). A similar survey in Texas, published just 2 years later, found that nearly 50% of licensed day-care centers had removed a least one child from their care due to behavior problems (Buck & Ambrosino, 2004).

Around this same time, researchers at Yale University Child Study Center sought to more systematically capture data at a national level (Gilliam, 2005). Using data from nearly 40,000 randomly selected classrooms in 52 state-funded prekindergarten systems, Walter Gilliam carefully weighted responses. During the 2002–2003 school year, on average, state-funded prekindergarten programs expelled 6.67 children per 1,000 enrolled. This would mean that approximately 5,117 children were expelled from prekindergarten programs nationwide. States varied widely in their rates of exclusion. Several states' rates were much higher. Maine, Alabama, and Delaware, all had rates well above 10 children per 1,000, and New Mexico's rate was highest, at 21.10 expulsions per 1,000 enrolled. At the other extreme, notably, Illinois teachers reported an expulsion rate of only 2.70 children per 1,000 served. By comparing individual state responses to their corresponding federally collected K–12 disciplinary data, the researchers were then able to calculate that preschoolers were expelled at a rate that is 3.20 times greater than the comparable rate for older students (which at the time was 2.09 per 1,000 enrolled). Although this study was a substantial methodological improvement over the early convenience sample surveys and provided our first rigorous national snapshot, results are only generalizable to public prekindergarten programs and don't capture the experiences of children in community-based child-care and preschool programs. Over time, studies have included different sectors of the early childhood system and have found increasingly concerning rates.

Building from his national survey, Gilliam next published (2007) results of a study using a smaller randomly selected sample of 119 classrooms serving preschool-age children (3- and 4-year-olds) in Massachusetts licensed child-care or public school-based programs. The sample included a mix of public and private schools, Head Starts, and for-profit and nonprofit child-care programs in urban, rural, and suburban parts of the state. As in the Illinois study, nearly 40% of teachers responding to this survey indicated that they had expelled at least one child in the prior 12 months (the 2001–2002 school year), and the researchers calculated the expulsion rate to be a staggering 27.42 children per 1,000 enrolled. This was nearly three times the rate Gilliam found among public prekindergarten programs in Massachusetts in his prior study and 34 times the rate of expulsions from Massachusetts K–12 schools.

Needless to say, these rates were shocking, and Gilliam's work was often cited in policy briefs and advocacy statements. Despite the attention, however, over a decade later, not much seems to have changed. In my first study of community-based child-care and preschool programs in Chicago neighborhoods (hereafter referred to as the Chicago area teacher study) we found a similar trend. Our results, published in the *Journal of Applied Developmental Psychology* (2019), showed that nearly 30% of teachers reported the expulsion of at least one child in the 2015–2016 school year, and 10% excluded three or more children. Focusing exclusively on home-based child-care programs, Alison Hooper and Claire Schweiker used nationally representative data collected as part of the 2012 National Survey of Early Care and Education and found that 13.3% reported having expelled at least one child in the last year.

Taking a different tack, researchers at the Center for American Progress used parent-reported data from a larger national data set to calculate expulsion rates. The 2016 National Survey of Children's Health surveys a nationally representative sample of parents about their children's health and health behaviors, including experiences in school and child care. Because data were collected from parents, rather than programs, a rate based on enrollment cannot be calculated, but this survey included a much broader array of programs and school settings than Gilliam's national sample nearly 15 years prior. Based on these data, the researchers estimated that over 50,000 preschoolers were suspended in 2016, and 17,000 children were expelled—more than three times the number estimated by Gilliam in 2005. When divided over the number of school days in the year, therefore, 250 preschoolers are excluded from U.S. preschools every day.

Looking across more than 20 years of research, we can draw several important conclusions. Exclusions are not relegated to only a small subset of programs, but instead are regular occurrences in between a quarter and a half of child-care and preschool programs across the country. Despite variations across studies, expulsion is a surprisingly common event in the lives of young children. Dozens of children in a neighborhood elementary school have likely experienced being excluded before they started kindergarten. Finally, children are more likely to be expelled during preschool than at any other point in their educational journey. Even with the more inclusive sampling techniques and nationally representative data, however, these reports do not tell the full story of early childhood exclusion. Missing from all of these studies are the thousands of children who have been informally excluded—pushed out of care but not formally expelled.

A Broad Definition of Exclusion

"They never said we couldn't come back but they made it impossible for us to stay." (Parent of 3-year old boy)

To fully understand the mechanisms, pathways, and costs of thousands of young children being removed from care each year in this country, we need an expansive definition of the ways they can be removed. Based on the K–12 model and DOE data collection mechanisms, the research literature tends to default into using the terms "expulsion" and "suspension" to describe permanent and temporary removals from early childhood care and education settings. While in some instances, these terms map onto early childhood policies and practices, in many other ways, they do not. Compulsory education laws in the United States dictate that there must be free and appropriate public education available for all school-age children in a district. Although some cities have made impressive advances toward universal preschool for 4-year-olds, in the vast majority of the country, there is no obligation to provide services for children under the age of 5, and thereby, there is no accountability. Because child care and preschool are treated as optional services, rather than education, many early childhood providers (a term I use interchangeably with "teacher" to refer to early childhood professionals, whether they work in classroom or home-based care settings) do not consider the removal of a child to be an expulsion and, many times, they are offended by the use of this term. Most of the studies cited above acknowledged this disconnect in designing their survey instruments, asking not "how many children did you expel" but instead "how many children were asked to leave your program due to challenging behaviors."

A kindergartner displaying severe challenging behaviors and who poses a risk to themselves, teachers, or other students would likely be evaluated for special education services and possibly transitioned into an alternative classroom or school setting. But down the street at a storefront child-care program, a child just a few months younger is not guaranteed a similar level of effort to accommodate their needs. Instead, the child's family may be told that the program "is not a good fit" for their child, and they should look elsewhere for care—an expulsion in all but name. Alternatively, the family could experience what some call a "soft expulsion"—practices that make the program not a viable or welcoming care arrangement for the family, leaving the family with little choice but to withdraw their child. For example, a program may repeatedly call parents to pick their child up early because of their behavior, forcing them to leave or miss work.

Whether a parent is told explicitly not to return or voluntarily withdraws their child to avoid repeated harassment and negative interactions, in all instances, the child is forced out of a setting to which they had grown accustomed and is subject to all of the well-documented immediate and long-term negative consequences associated with suspension and expulsion—lost learning time, lost or soured relationships, lost family income from missed work, etc. In this text, therefore, I use the terms "exclusion" and "expulsion" somewhat interchangeably. "Exclusion" may better encompass both the formal and informal ways that children who have displayed difficult or challenging behaviors are asked or told or encouraged to leave a care arrangement. At the same time, the term "expulsion" has the cultural gravitas needed to draw attention to this crisis.

As limited as the data on formal expulsions and suspensions in early childhood are, there are almost no empirical data on soft expulsions or push-outs. In one recent study, we attempted to collect reports from administrators on the number of children with challenging behavior problems who were voluntarily dis-enrolled because the program could not meet the child's needs. Across two samples, we found that the number of voluntarily dis-enrolled children was three times that of the formally expelled children. Said another way, while administrators reported a comparatively low rate of 2.07 expulsions per 1,000 children enrolled, rates of push-outs were above 6 per 1,000 enrolled, and a sizable subsample of programs saw 14 of every 1,000 served leave voluntarily. We will discuss this study in greater detail in

Chapter 9, but I mention this finding early to emphasize further the importance of not letting children fall through the cracks simply because their exclusion was not formally labeled an expulsion.

Regardless of the method of exclusion, these practices deprive children of valuable early learning experiences and place them at risk of disengagement and diminished educational opportunities. Successive exclusions also have cumulative and compounding impacts on children and their families. Especially in areas of limited options for care, each exclusion further narrows a family's choices for affordable, accessible, and appropriate care for their child. As we saw in the example of Lance, repeated exclusions can place a child at substantial risk of attending lower-quality and unsafe care arrangements.

Who Gets Expelled?

At all grades and ages, Black children, particularly boys, are disproportionately excluded from school through suspensions and expulsions. Black preschoolers are twice as likely as Latino and White preschoolers, and over five times more likely than Asian American preschoolers, to be expelled (Malik, 2017). Even though Black children make up only 18% of children in public preschool nationwide, they make up 48% of those receiving multiple suspensions in a given year (U.S. Department of Education Office of Civil Rights, 2014). Likewise, while boys constitute 51% of children in preschool, they receive 82% of suspensions and expulsions (Malik, 2017). These trends mirror those in grade school and beyond. In public K–12 settings, Black students comprise only 15% of all U.S. students but make up 36% of those expelled and 44% of students with more than one suspension (U.S. Department of Education Office of Civil Rights, 2014). Notably, these disparities have grown over time, while discipline rates have decreased for Latino, Asian, American Indian, and White students from 1991 to 2005, they increased for Black youth (Wallace et al., 2008).

Further, while boys are suspended in greater numbers than girls, and Black boys are suspended more than three times as often as White boys, Black girls are six times more likely to be suspended than their White female peers and represent the fastest-growing populations in the juvenile justice system (Crenshaw et al., 2015). Only 20 percent of female preschoolers in public school programs in 2013–2014 were Black, but Black girls made up 54 percent of female preschool children with one or more suspensions. Some studies of grade-school-age children have found that Hispanic/Latino children are over-represented among those being disciplined (Raffeaele Mendez & Knoff, 2003), but the findings are not consistent (e.g., Gordon et al., 2000). However, one of the first studies to explicitly examine this in a national preschool-age sample (Zeng et al., 2019) did show that Hispanic/Latino children are more likely to be suspended and expelled than their peers. Given the rapid growth of this demographic among children under the age of 5, the authors indicate that this trend is very concerning. The persistent comorbidity of disproportional rates of removal for children of color and racially disparate performances on achievement tests have led some to consider the U.S. achievement and discipline gaps as two sides of the same coin.

Within the early childhood literature, another consistent characteristic of excluded children is that they are older. Gilliam and Shahar first pointed to this trend in their 2006 Massachusetts study discussed above, showing that expulsions were more common in classrooms of 4-year-olds than in classrooms of 3-year-olds. More recent child-level data from a population study using parent reports by Songtian Zeng and colleagues at the University of Massachusetts Boston and the University of Illinois at Urbana-Champaign confirmed this trend, showing that 50% of suspended or expelled children were 4 years old, while only 13% were 3. At the same time, it is important to note that data on exclusions of infants and toddlers are very scarce.

In studies of K–12 suspension and expulsion, the odds of being removed from school are increased for children with diagnosed disabilities. This increased risk is prevalent across all racial groups (Krezmien et al., 2006) but is particularly high for some combinations, specifically, speech/language delays, emotional disturbances, and learning disabilities. In their review of nearly a decade of expulsion and suspension data from Kansas public schools, Krezmien and colleagues found that African American students with an emotional disturbance diagnosis were more likely to be expelled than any other racial or disability combination group. Based on data from the U.S. DOE's Office of Civil Rights reports, public preschools do not appear to be excluding preschool-age students with disabilities at disproportionate rates. Children with disabilities (those served by the Individuals with Disabilities Education Act) represent 22% of preschool enrollment, 19% of the students suspended once, and 17% of the students suspended more than once. It is important to remember, however, that many disabilities, especially those related to learning behaviors, are diagnosed later, when a child's reading and writing abilities can be assessed using standardized diagnostic tools.

Parallel data on disability status and discipline experiences are limited for non-public-school settings. In fact, during a systematic review of early childhood expulsion literature, we found that only two studies that included measures of children's learning differences or disability status (Zinsser et al., 2022). In one study, by Zeng and colleagues, children with attention deficit hyperactivity disorder (ADHD) were more likely to be expelled, but those with learning disabilities were less likely to be expelled. Other diagnoses, such as autism, speech-language delays, or internalizing problems like anxiety, were not statistically associated with expulsion. In their evaluation of a pilot program for children at risk of expulsion from child care, Deborah Perry and colleagues (2008) provide greater detail about the types of diagnoses and needs among excluded children. Specifically, of those referred, 19% had at least one previously established diagnosis, with the most common being speech-language delay, ADHD, and sensory impairment. In my own work surveying administrators, we have found that of those who reported at least one expulsion, a third expelled at least one child with a diagnosed disability and 10% only excluded children with such diagnoses. A year later, when that same sample was surveyed using more inclusive categories of exclusion and child-level demographics, we found that although 12.5% of excluded children had a disability, these children were over-represented among those voluntarily withdrawn from programs. That is to say, children with developmental needs and disabilities were more often pushed out than formally expelled.

Until now, I have been working hard to avoid addressing the question of "Why?" Why are very young children being expelled from preschool and child care? What could a 2-year-old possibly be doing that would justify kicking them out? My intentional avoidance of the why question up until now stems from my agreement with Walter Gilliam's familiar refrain, "Expulsion is not a child behavior, it is an adult decision" (Gilliam & Shahar, 2006). It should not matter what a child is "doing" because, especially in early childhood, they are not entirely responsible for their behavior. My position as a community and applied development psychologist necessitates that I look upward in the ecological model of human development to consider not what the child did to cause his own expulsion, but what the adults, schools, and policymakers *did not do* to retain and support him.

To start this book with a recitation of the faults in young children, their shortcomings and transgressions that sealed their fates, would be to fall into the trap of what William Ryan coined "blaming the victim." In his 1971 book, Ryan was reacting to dominant social theories at the time that attempted to divert responsibility for the plight of poor people and people of color in the United States away from structural racism and 300 years of racism and inequity and toward the cultural and behavioral patterns of the poor—namely, blaming the low achievement of Black children in school on absent fathers and unwed mothers. Despite nearly 50 years of discourse on victim-blaming, our society still holds children, especially Black children, as partially or fully responsible for the transgressions committed against them, such as expulsion and incarceration.

To push back on the dominant perception of expulsion being caused by pathological shortcomings of individual children, we will carefully explore the broader contextual and intra-personal factors that result in some adults centering behavior problems "in" particular children (e.g., Mavropoulou & Padeliadu, 2002). Moving forward, we will explore what types of behaviors are viewed as problematic or challenging by early childhood educators and the varied and complex roots of these perceptions and behaviors.

3

A Challenge for Whom?

Elijah, a 4-year-old, Black boy, had been at Rainbow Bridge Learning Center for over a year. Although both of his parents worked, their income was low enough that Elijah, like nearly 80% of children at the center, qualified for tuition assistance from the state in the form of vouchers. In the prior year, the center had gotten to know Elijah's family well, as they had worked to understand and support him through some explosive tantrums. By observing his behavior and talking frequently with the family, teachers in the 3-year-old classroom had determined that Elijah's distress at lunch time was primarily in reaction to the various foods touching each other. The program purchased special plates with divided sections and almost immediately his tantrums subsided and he finished out the school year smoothly. But upon returning in the fall, teachers in the Blue room noticed that very quickly Elijah began displaying erratic, aggressive behaviors (e.g., biting) throughout the day. The staff struggled to calm him down and he would escalate quickly once frustrated, throwing things and attempting to run out of the building.

Ms. Elena, the center director, and the teachers were very aware of the likely root causes of Elijah's behavior—he was exhausted and hungry. Over the summer, his mother had taken a job working nights and Elijah refused to go to sleep without her. Ms. Elena described it as "some kind of sleep phobia." He would fight sleep until his mom returned home from work around 1 a.m. At school, Elijah refused to nap and increasingly refused to eat. By November 2019, except for the occasional sip of orange juice, he was going for 10 hours without food. During nap time he was "bouncing off the walls and other children's cots . . . it just got worse and worse." Even with complete empathy and understanding of the causes, the teaching staff at Rainbow Bridge did not know what to do. It occurred to Elena that Elijah may do well on a part-time schedule, allowing him to sleep at home in the morning and eat a meal with his mother before attending preschool in the afternoon. Unfortunately, because of the funding requirements, Rainbow Bridge could not enroll him just in the afternoons. Ms. Elena reached out to neighboring programs and found one willing to enroll him and even offered a partial scholarship since they did not accept the child-care assistance program vouchers. This looked like a viable solution, and Ms. Elena set up a meeting between the family and the new program and began the process of dis-enrolling Elijah. Unfortunately, the week after Elijah started at his new program, his father lost his job, and the family could no longer afford the remaining balance of the tuition. Reflecting on the series of events, Ms. Elena admitted that she was too quick to push him out. "I really messed up . . . we just could not handle [him]. I know it is very distressing on the parents too."

As much as she regrets the fact that Elijah is not receiving the type of care that he needs most, Ms. Elena knows that she ultimately made the right choice to try to transition him out of her program. She described the palpable difference in the air of the Blue room with Elijah's departure. "We're calm now. We can really focus on the other children." In the prior few months, everyone had become almost hardened off; even the children had stopped reacting to the outbursts. Even more concerning, she reported that "in the Blue room, we were finding that other kids were copying this behavior because it was the only way to get attention."

***

The Challenge with Challenging Behavior

Teachers consistently report children's challenging or problematic behavior as the most common reason for pursuing expulsion. Despite this concordance, definitions of challenging or problematic behaviors are less consistent. Some definitions may point to unwanted behaviors that are repeated over a period of time, ones that interfere with the child's ability to play, learn, and get along with others, or ones that cannot be mollified by developmentally appropriate instruction or guidance. All of these definitions leave a lot up to individual interpretation. While some behaviors pose a significant threat, like hitting and biting, others are more subjective. Across multiple studies that inquired about specific concerning behaviors preceding a child's expulsion, preschool teachers often cited problems such as being disrespectful or defiant, using inappropriate language, yelling, or screaming (Bee, 2012; Martin et al., 2018; Hoover & Stainback-Tracy, 2007; Perry et al., 2008). In my Chicago area preschool teacher study, participants were just as likely to cite children's disruptive behaviors like yelling, uncontrollable crying, and being too clingy as overtly dangerous behaviors and the reason for requesting that a child be expelled.

It is this subjectivity that is at the heart of Gilliam's refrain about expulsions being an adult decision. It is ultimately an adult who is challenged by a child's behavior. From the perspective of a young child, the challenge is their loss of control, their loss of agency, or their significant uncontrollable emotions. A 2-year-old may bite a playmate for many reasons: because they are teething and the pain is making them irritable; because someone took their toy and they do not yet have the language abilities to express how that made them feel; because they are so upset and are unable to self-soothe, but using their teeth is a reliable way to get an adult to intervene and help them calm down. A young child's defiance or lashing out is an automatic reaction to their emotions and their circumstances. As such, young children's behaviors cannot be categorized as problematic or challenging in the absence of a deeper understanding of their developmental stage and abilities, temperament, relationships, and environment. At the same time, attention must be paid to the attributes, experiences, and perceptions of the person interpreting the child's behaviors.

Many of the behaviors labeled as "challenging" are developmentally appropriate and dissipate with time. More than half of preschoolers who display concerning levels of aggression or who struggle with impulse control will no longer exhibit these behaviors at kindergarten entry (Shaw et al., 2000). Challenging behaviors are also ubiquitous—most early childhood classrooms will have at least one child who is experiencing significant social, emotional, or behavioral needs (Egger & Angold, 2006) which could manifest as noncompliance, aggression, or destruction of property. Without intervention and support, children who display these behaviors struggle to form positive relationships with peers and teachers and miss out on academic and social-emotional learning opportunities. Over time, low social-emotional competence, often thought of as both a precursor to and result of many challenging behaviors, can hinder a child's cognitive development, relationships with family members and peers, and future mental health (Heckman, 2006; Jones et al., 2015; Shonkoff et al., 2012). In addition to placing them at risk for school exclusion, such behaviors are also correlated with the long-term outcomes described in the preceding chapter, like delinquency.

Given how commonplace and developmentally expected behaviors such as these are in early childhood settings, you may ask, why are children disciplined so harshly? An important contextual factor to remember is that when a teacher is faced with a child biting, throwing chairs, inconsolably screaming, or otherwise disrupting the classroom, she is not just trying to figure out the best way to handle the situation to meet the needs of that individual child. She must also consider the safety and experience of the 18 other children in the classroom, all while maintaining her own emotional and physical well-being. The risks to teachers' personal safety are not to be passed over.

Across nearly a dozen years of conducting interviews and focus groups with early educators, I have heard many stories about teachers being seriously injured in the classroom. One teacher recounted being bitten so hard while trying to shield one child from another that she needed stitches. A teacher in Virginia was concussed after being struck in the face by a flying chair. At Rainbow Bridge, Ms. Elena recounted that in a single year, her teachers filed three workman's compensation claims for injuries caused by children, including one teacher who had her wrist broken. Altogether, the claims would raise Ms. Elena's insurance premiums by $5,000 per year. She lamented to me, "Our premiums will not be reassessed for another three years. That's $15,000 extra in insurance. We're a nonprofit. Where is that money going to come from?" As aware and sympathetic as Ms. Elena is to the need to provide proper care and support for children, especially those who struggle behaviorally, there are real physical and financial implications for teachers and programs.

Beyond the physical risk that children's challenging behaviors can pose, countless studies have demonstrated the emotional toll that such behaviors have on our educators. As we will discuss in more detail in a later chapter, teachers report that managing children's challenging behaviors contributes significantly to job-related stress, decreases their enjoyment and satisfaction with their jobs, and generally detracts from their well-being (Friedman-Krauss et al., 2014; Hoover et al., 2012; Quesenberry et al., 2014). Administrators also report observing the adverse effects of behavior management on staff and that inadequate supports for child behavior contribute to higher turnover rates among teachers (Conners Edge et al., 2018; Vinh et al., 2016). Teachers also consistently report being inadequately trained in managing challenging behaviors (Friedman-Krauss et al., 2014; Yoshikawa & Zigler, 2000); the available training tends to focus on reactive approaches, such as restraint and time-out techniques, as opposed to proactive social-emotional skill building (Quesenberry et al., 2014; US DHHS and US DOE, 2014). Without understanding the root developmental and environmental sources of children's behavior and without adequate supports and opportunities to reflect on classroom practices, it is not surprising that children who do not conform with or facilitate a calm classroom environment are labeled as "challenging."

Elijah's behavior challenged his teachers' abilities to create a calm learning environment. His tantrums, resistance to napping, and noncompliance were demanding substantial attention from them, and they were quickly losing patience and running out of energy. As is the case for many children who display behaviors that challenge early childhood teachers, Elijah's distress at school can be seen as a reaction to challenges or stress in some other area of his life. Even with insight into Elijah's home life cultivated over the preceding year, the teachers at Rainbow Bridge were not fully aware of, or able to account for, the cumulative toll that his family's financial situation and his mother's shifting work schedule had taken on the young boy.

As First Lady Barbara Bush observed in her campaign for family literacy, parents are children's first teachers. As such, when teachers understand a child's home life, they are better able to support their learning at school. Especially in early childhood, family well-being is a strong predictor of children's academic and behavioral success. When families thrive and are healthy, children blossom. However, when parents struggle, for example, with mental health or substance use issues, children display higher rates of behavioral and academic challenges. Children with higher levels of exposure to adversities at home are more likely to be diagnosed with disabilities and mental and behavior disorders themselves, which increases their risk of being excluded from school. So what are these adversities that can place children on the road to exclusion? How pervasive are they, and how exactly do they result in challenging behaviors in the preschool classroom?

Adverse childhood experiences (sometimes called ACEs) are broadly defined as potentially stressful or traumatic events that occur in a child's family or social environment and may cause harm or distress, and that have long-term effects on a person's development, health, and well-being. ACEs not only include all forms of physical and emotional maltreatment, such as sexual abuse, neglect, and exploitation, but also include experiences such as witnessing domestic violence, parental divorce or incarceration, and caregiver alcohol or drug or substance abuse disorders.

Much of our understanding of the breadth and depth of childhood adversity comes from national surveys like the National Survey of Children's Health. In a 2016 report using these parent-reported data and published by Child Trends (childtrends.org), overall exposure rates are staggering—46%

of American children under the age of 18 had experienced at least one ACE. Some adversities are more prevalent than others. A quarter of children in the National Survey of Children's Health lived in economic hardship, or had parents who were separated or divorced. A smaller but not insubstantial portion lived with someone who struggled with a severe mental illness (8%) or substance addiction (9%), or was suicidal. A similar proportion (8%) had a parent who was incarcerated. The more directly detrimental adversities were somewhat less frequent; between 3% and 5% of children in this nationally representative sample had witnessed domestic violence, had been the victim of violence themselves, or had experienced the death of a parent.

Compared to these national estimates, rates of ACEs among children who have been excluded from care are substantially higher. In our fall 2019 survey, we asked nearly 100 Illinois early childhood administrators to describe the children who were being asked to leave their program due to challenging behavior, including whether they suspected the children had experienced any of the commonly cited ACEs. These administrators described high rates of adversity among the children excluded in the preceding year, with children on average having over 2.60 ACEs (SD = 2.12). Across the board, there were high rates of divorce (50%), parental unemployment (51.10%), food (36.20%) and housing insecurity (28.30%), and parental incarceration (22.9%). Children also frequently witnessed (42.20%) or were themselves the victim of violence (39.9%) or had spent time in foster care (14.9%).

These alarming rates of adversity, drawn from a small convenience sample, are somewhat higher than, but not inconsistent with, data from a more systematic, nationally representative study. In 2019, Songtian Zeng and colleagues published a study in *Child Abuse & Neglect* examining the association between children's experiences of adversity and their risk of expulsion from preschool. Using parent-reported data on a sample of over 6,000 children drawn from the National Survey of Children's Health data collected in 2016, these researchers found significant differences in rates of adversity between children excluded and those retained in child-care and preschool programs across the country. For example, excluded children were more likely to live in poverty, witness domestic violence, or live with a parent who struggles with mental illness or substance abuse than children who were retained, even after controlling for child age, race, and gender. The authors of this study further determined the odds of a child being excluded from care based on their experiences of adversity. For each adverse experience a child had had, their chance of being suspended or expelled increased by

80%. Children were at particularly high risk of being excluded if they were exposed to domestic violence, severe mental illness, substance abuse, or were the victim of violence. Odds were also elevated if they had lived in high poverty, had divorced parents, or had a parent who was incarcerated. Zeng and colleagues conclude that the cumulative experiences of adversity place children under extreme stress, which negatively affects children's behaviors at school. Unfortunately, as was well documented in the 2016 Risk and Reach Report (Erikson Institute, 2019), communities that have high concentrations of risk indicators, such as poverty, drug overdose deaths, maltreatment, and homelessness, are also those with the lowest concentrations of high-quality, affordable child care. Children who have faced adversity, especially poverty, are often served by community child-care programs that are of lower quality and are least well prepared to support their behavior. In one study, researchers found that children from low-income families tended to have teachers who were observed to be less sensitive, harsher, and more punitive compared to teachers in centers serving more advantaged families. Even when programs are fortunate enough to have access to behavioral resources and supports, a child's expulsion can prevent a family from accessing those meaningful supports.

Beyond the obvious statement that children should not experience such hardships and adversities, there is ample evidence of the long-term deleterious effects of these early life experiences. Children with higher ACE scores are more likely to be diagnosed with physical and mental disabilities, including increased rates of behavior disorders (Hunt et al., 2017), anxiety, and depression (Rose et al., 2014), and perform more poorly on assessments of language, literacy, and math abilities in early childhood than children experiencing fewer or no adversities. Teachers also rate children who have faced adversity as more aggressive and poorer at regulating their emotions and engagement with tasks (Lipscomb et al., 2021) . Because you cannot run a controlled experimental study of the effects of ACEs, however, we cannot wholeheartedly say whether ACEs are the reason children experience these challenges and, most likely, it is a much more complicated story. That is to say, not only does early adversity put children at risk of developing learning difficulties and behavioral needs, but also the genetic predisposition to develop mental health needs is itself linked to the adversity of living with parents with major depression. Further, although many studies of ACEs statistically control for children's race, socioeconomic status, and gender, not all do, and children's access to the supports and resources that would mitigate the effects of adversity on their development is going to vary across racial and economic lines.

What research has demonstrated, however, is that exposure to prolonged adversities such as physical or emotional abuse or prolonged economic hardship during early childhood can alter and disrupt the development of a child's brain and other organ systems. The cumulative effect of prolonged, intense, or frequent adversities triggers the toxic stress response. In extreme cases, such as chronic abuse, especially during early periods of brain development, regions of the brain involved in the processing and experience of fear and anxiety, as well as regions related to impulsive responses, overproduce synaptic connections between neurons. This experience-dependent response is the brain's mechanism to adapt its growth to best suit the environment the child is living in. Prolonged exposure to an unsafe living condition results in a brain that is braced for sudden, stressful, and harmful events—on high alert and able to respond quickly to any perceived threat. At the same time, this same brain may show fewer neural connections in regions associated with reasoning and planning because, in times of active threat, planning is less critical than preserving immediate safety. In a 2020 interview, the comedian Hannah Gatsby was asked whether her tough childhood impacted her dreams. She laughed and said, "There are no dreams; that's trauma, isn't it?" She went on to describe how, as a homeless rape survivor and living with undiagnosed autism, this meant that she was narrowly focused on just barely getting through each day. There was no thinking toward the future, planning her career, or dreaming. Her brain was hard-wired to survive.

While trauma at any age is egregious, the neural networks for coping with stress are particularly malleable or sensitive during early childhood. Early exposures to stress not only shape these networks to be more sensitive and respond at even lower thresholds, but also alters the hormonal systems that help slow or turn off the response when the threat is removed. Children who have experienced toxic levels of stress, therefore, may feel threatened by a situation where no real threat exists—such as perceiving someone else as angry or hostile when their face is neutral—and they may remain excessively anxious or on edge long after the perceived threat has been removed. In the classroom, a child may perceive an accidental jostle on the playground as an intentional push, react impulsively and aggressively, and then remain in a heightened state of arousal through lunch and nap time. The morning's agitation would interrupt his ability to eat and rest, only heightening his dysregulation for the afternoon. In the short term, this child's heightened vigilance will distract him from learning. He spends circle time actively scanning children's faces for negative emotions, avoids collaborative play in the block corner, and cannot focus his attention during story time. Sustained activation of the stress response system can also chemically damage the hippocampus, the area of the brain that is critical to learning and memory, ever widening the achievement gap. Playing this scenario out, this little boy likely would have had similar reactions to perceived threats on the playground on multiple occasions. Without insightful, supportive reactions from adults to help him calm down and feel safe, work by Zheng and others implies that he would likely be expelled. What is perhaps most unfair about this scenario is that when a child experiencing high levels of toxic stress is expelled, they are likely being sent home to spend even more time in a potentially dangerous, caustic setting. If the home is not safe, the child has been relegated away from interactions with mandated reporters who could be our front-line identifiers of instances of neglect and abuse.

At the same time, not all children who are asked to leave care arrangements have experienced multiple ACEs, if any at all. Further, experiencing early trauma is not deterministic—these experiences are associated with increased risks but do not guarantee that a child will later develop a severe mental or physical health problem. Early experiences of positivity and environments that reduce the toxicity of stress can significantly bolster an individual child's resilience and health.

In the case of Elijah, he was thankfully not in a dangerous setting, but his body was under a great deal of stress. Refusing to eat, fighting off sleep, and experiencing the emotional pain of separation from his mother overnight was likely triggering similar hormonal responses by Elijah's body as those described above. Coupled with the intermittent financial distress and changing schedules and family dynamics, it is understandable that this little boy was having a hard time, and that unfortunately is not an anomaly.

Nationwide, experiences of adversity are highly concentrated in subpopulations of children. Put bluntly, Black children like Elijah are substantially more likely to witness violence, live in poverty, and be the victims of abuse at an early age than their White peers. A 2016 study published in the journal *Pediatrics* reported that by age 4, 1 in 10 Black children would have at least one confirmed case of maltreatment reported to child protective services, whereas that number is only 1 in 20 for 4-year-old White children. Black children are much more likely to have three or more ACEs than their non-Hispanic White peers and Hispanic peers. Rates for multiple adversities among Hispanic and non-Hispanic White children are relatively comparable (10–11%), but non-Hispanic White children are more likely to have experienced no adversities (59%) compared to their Hispanic (48%) and Black (36%) peers. Due to centuries of structural racism in this country, we unfortunately now have substantial evidence of the intergenerational transmission of toxic stress as well. At the intersection of neuroscience, epigenetics, sociology, and developmental psychology, researchers are assessing how social conditions produce adversities that generate toxic stress. What is increasingly clear from the evidence is that growing up under extreme stress leaves a mark on children's developing brains. Early cognitive and behavioral challenges stemming from this adversity are associated with poorer educational and occupational attainment, which recapitulates the economic and social adversities for the next generation.

A simplistic interpretation of these frequencies would be that early childhood programs disproportionately expel Black children because they are biologically predisposed through generations of trauma and adversity to display impulsive, aggressive, and inappropriate behavior. This was, for years, the predominant hypothesis in the study of school discipline. Researchers commonly hypothesized that Black children might actually engage in more frequent and severe rule-breaking behaviors, explaining why they are removed from school at a higher rate than their non-Black peers. However, in critiques of the available evidence, Petras and colleagues (2011) and others have argued that the reliance on correlational evidence and office records of disciplinary action is insufficiently rigorous. This approach to understanding discipline disparities fails to look outside of the child and family unit. There is some recognition that structural racism has created the conditions that contribute to children's stress levels underlying their behavior, but the majority of the "blame" is still placed in the biology of the individual child and his family.

Modern analytical techniques are lending us to increasingly acknowledge the multiple interacting factors contributing to children's behavior. Although the effects of structural racism on children's early cognitive and emotional development cannot be discounted, it is important to also consider which factors outside of the individual child contribute to their removal—for example, discriminatory differences in perceptions of them and their behavior. One longitudinal study of over 1,000 first graders showed that Black children in poverty were at the highest risk of removal, even after controlling for children's early individual levels of aggression and disruption. In this study, racial group differences in the severity or frequency of disruptive or dangerous behavior did not explain the disparities in removals. Put more simply, Black children were not behaving any differently than White children; they were just more likely to be disciplined harshly.

Researchers have documented that across ages and settings, teachers perceive Black boys as more defiant and disruptive than other groups of children (Newcomb et al., 2002; Wentzel, 2002). However, observational studies find that the frequency of such "disruptive" behaviors does not differ by race; Black students do not engage in more severe or more frequent disruptive or dangerous behaviors (Skiba et al., 2011). Regardless, Black middle schoolers are referred to the office more often than their White peers for offenses that have a high degree of subjectivity in interpretation, such as "disrespect" or "loitering" (Skiba et al., 2002). They then receive harsher levels of punishment for less severe behaviors than other children, a reflection of administrators' racial biases (Gregory & Weinstein, 2008). As we will see in the next chapter, a very similar trend is emerging in studies of early care and education settings.

As any parent knows, children's behavior can really challenge adults' emotions. The high-pitch screams, incessant mess, and whining are things we must endure daily. As children grow older and develop better language and regulation skills, the tantrums often naturally subside. However, for many children, this transition is not as precipitous as parents and teachers may wish. Upwards of 20% of typically developing children, and between 30% and 70% of children with disabilities, routinely display behaviors that teachers describe as "challenging."

When children are "challenging," they are naturally reacting to their environment with whatever skills and resources they have at their disposal. Young children are not purposefully acting in destructive, harmful ways in order to upset their teachers or parents. Instead of viewing challenging behaviors as intentional manipulation, it can be helpful to reframe them as a young child's efforts to communicate. Even as an adult, I am guilty of getting so upset that I struggle to communicate clearly and calmly, and I have full command of the English language. Two-, 3-, and 4-year-old children are still acquiring both the vocabulary to articulate their needs and the regulatory skills to manage their feelings enough to communicate effectively. Even in the absence of prior adversity, it is developmentally appropriate for children to act out behaviorally when they cannot communicate their needs. That is not to dismiss the fact that teachers are legitimately distressed, exhausted, and at times afraid of being injured.

Rather than normalizing children's social and emotional learning process, however, we refer to bumps along the road of this learning process as "challenging." If 20% of children in a school had peanut allergies and the school still allowed peanut butter to be served in the cafeteria, parents, pediatricians, and politicians would all be outraged. They would demand structural reform, including changes in school policies and training for staff on how to safely assist children experiencing allergic reactions. In reality, peanut allergies are estimated to affect only 1.4% of children in the United States, a rate 14 times lower than the incidence of challenging behavior. And yet, child-care programs, camps, and schools across the country routinely ban nut-based snacks from their buildings and keep EpiPens on hand. We do not blame children for being allergic to peanuts, but we do blame them for needing help managing their emotions. This is not to deny the fact that it is tough to be around an emotional, combative, destructive child, but the time has come to flip the script. Rather than talking about the children's behavior as challenging, it is time to consider how our perceptions of children's behavior, especially Black children's behavior, are problematic or deficient.

4

Biased Perceptions of and Responses to Behavior

Kaia Roller, a Black kindergartener attending a charter elementary school, was arrested by Police Officer Dennis Turner in September 2019 in Orlando, Florida. According to news reports and interviews with her mother, Kaia was arrested for having a temper tantrum in her classroom. She lost control of her body and swung wildly with hands and feet, striking the assistant principal, who was trying to restrain her. The assistant principal wanted to press charges against the girl for kicking her, and the school's resources officer called for a transporter officer to respond to the front office. In the officer's body camera video posted online by the family's attorney, you can see that when the responding officer arrives, Kaia is sitting calmly with a teacher, reading a book. Officer Turner orders Kaia to stand up and puts plastic zip ties around her wrists. You hear in the background other teaching staff questioning the need for the restraints. Kaia begins to cry and asks, "What are those for?" not understanding what is happening. When a teacher later questions Turner's use of the restraints directly, he responds, "If she were bigger, she'd be wearing regular handcuffs," adding that he had arrested a 7-year-old earlier that day. Even though no charges were ever officially filed and Kaia was soon home with her parents, she went through juvenile processing, had her mug shot taken, and was fingerprinted. The hysterical crying pervasive in the video lingers in your mind long after the video ends, but only begins to indicate how distressing this event was for Kaia.

* * *

If you are like me, reading this account likely filled you with emotions and questions. How could someone have thought this was a good idea? Why did no one intervene and stop the arrest of a kindergartener for being upset? What did this experience teach poor little Kaia? How is she ever going to feel safe at school again? What are the underlying perceptions, relationships, systems, and processes that triggered this series of events?

As we saw in the previous chapter, Kaia's intense emotional reaction should be familiar to anyone who works with young children. Upwards of 20% of 2- to 5-year-olds are estimated to display challenging behaviors, and for children with disabilities, the rate is 3 to 7 times higher (Hemmeter et al., 2016). It is evident that the numerous adults involved in this episode also perceived Kaia and her behavior very differently from one another. Based on reporting by the *Washington Post*, Kaia's emotional outburst only became physical when the assistant principal tried to restrain her. The administrator's desire to press charges implies that she perceived Kaia's actions as intentional—that Kaia was purposefully harming her and represented a persistent threat to her personal safety.

Further, the attempt to restrain Kaia implies that the administrator believed that her emotional outburst was inherently problematic, rather than a natural reaction to being exhausted from a poor night's sleep (as her mother reported later). In comparison, the teacher calmly reading a book with Kaia does not seem to share these same beliefs. Rather than posing a physical threat, this teacher is treating Kaia as a young child who needs the supportive attention of a caring adult to help her calm down and prepare to return to the classroom. Perhaps it is the result of training and experience working with young children that enable her to perceive Kaia as a child deserving of emotional support and essentially innocent.

With the entrance of the arresting officer, we are introduced to another contrasting perception of this young girl. That is, a grown man with 23 years of experience as a police officer and prior military service perceived the 45-pound grade-school student to pose such a significant threat to his personal safety that she needed to be physically restrained in zip ties. Of course, it cannot go unsaid that this scenario and each actor's perceptions are couched within the social and historical contexts of our time, including structural racism and the "adultification" of Black children (Dumas & Nelson, 2016). Further, the different actors' perceptions are dependent on their internal states—levels of stress, sensitivity to perceived threats, and sense of responsibility in a context. I do not provide these qualifiers as a way to excuse the traumatization of Kaia, but rather to frame the depth of the discussion forthcoming. In this chapter, we will begin to unpack these processes and perceptual biases that lead adults to make decisions that result in children being excluded from care. In line with the ecological model of human development, the expulsion process is occurring at multiple levels simultaneously. Children, parents, teachers, and administrators all experience the expulsion process differently. Each brings to the process their own biases, needs, beliefs, and goals that drive their behavior and influence their interpretation of others' behaviors.

Implicit Biases

Given the staggering disparities we described previously, central to the process of exclusion are adults' biased perceptions of children and their behavior. Biases can be explicit or implicit, and both types will affect our understanding of situations, actions, and decision-making in daily life.

Explicit biases are those that are conscious to the individual and are often overtly stated, such as a teacher saying to a child's parent that they prefer to have more girls in their class because they are "easy" or "more fun." This explicit preference for girls will play out in the classroom in numerous ways, ranging from the way behaviors are perceived to the way teachers react. For example, children caught running to the art table may be treated very differently by this teacher based on their gender. A girl may be perceived as being "enthusiastic about engaging in learning" and be greeted with a smile. On the other hand, a boy caught running may be perceived as "dangerous" and receive a consequence of sitting on the calm-down-spot. The teacher may further view the boy's inability to behave as a fixed trait and, therefore, not invest time or effort into trying to guide his decision-making and inhibitory control. Conversely, girls in the classroom may receive direct instruction, reinforcement, and multiple chances to make better choices and regulate their behavior.

Implicit biases refer to unconscious or automatic attitudes or stereotypes. Everyone is susceptible to these biases, which are activated involuntarily without an individual's awareness or voluntary control (Rudman, 2004). Positive and negative unconscious feelings and attitudes about people develop at a very early age through direct and indirect messaging. Implicit biases are the outcome of a lifetime of cultural conditioning. We acquire them over time through our consumption of media, and by observing how members of your family and social group treat and interact with people of other social groups. That is, we attribute positive and desirable qualities with some identities, and harmful or undesirable qualities with others. In the United States, the most pervasive of these biases fall along racial lines. As Kenneth and Mamie Clark demonstrated over 80 years ago in their infamous doll study, these biases develop very early in life and exist across identity groups. When offered a choice, both Black and White children as young as 5 universally chose the White doll to play with because it looked "pretty and good," while the Black doll looked "bad and dirty" (Clark & Clark, 1939).

Beyond the selection of toys, these implicit biases influence individual behaviors and decision-making, which can result in inequitable outcomes for different groups. The same scenario described above could play out in a classroom with a teacher who is implicitly biased toward girls. Just as above, this teacher could reprimand a boy's energetic behavior and reinforce a girl's identical behavior. What is so dangerous about implicit bias is that it is an unconscious process. Because we are not fully aware of our perceptions, they are less controllable.

As has long been the mantra of early childhood education, teachers strive to see and support the development of the "whole child." With regard to the curriculum, this typically means attending to physical and social-emotional health, in addition to academic preparedness. Ideally, teachers are additionally attending to multiple aspects of children's lives and seeing them as the rich, socially complex people that they are. Generally, knowing multiple aspects of a child's identity can benefit many aspects of teaching—knowing about a family's traditions or a parent's occupation allows teachers to relate classroom materials to a child's home life. At the same time, seeing the "whole child" means that teachers can unconsciously fall back on intersecting biases. While there are numerous implicit biases at play in the American education system, three, in particular, have been pointed toward as contributing to disparities in early childhood expulsion: being a boy, being Black,[1] and being big. The more these "3 Bs" describe an individual child, the greater extent to which adults' perceptions and behaviors are biased against that child, and the more likely they are to be excluded from care.

In our 2016 study of Chicago area preschool teachers, we posed the question in a follow-up interview, "According to data from the U.S. Department of Education, boys are more likely to be expelled from preschool than girls, why do you think that is?" While some teachers explicitly called out our society's

[1] Although our society at large holds numerous biases and racism has been shown to significantly and negatively affect children from multiple backgrounds, the preponderance of evidence in the early childhood education expulsion literature points toward anti-Black bias. In our systematic review of the literature, we found only one study of ECE expulsion and suspension (Zeng et al., 2020) which reported disproportionate rates of expulsion of Hispanic/Latino children (in addition to Black children) as compared to their White peers. Likewise, disproportionality in K–12 studies of expulsion primarily falls along Black/White lines. Thus, in this chapter, I focus on biases against Black children.

reliance on sexist stereotypes, over a quarter of the sample replied in ways that demonstrate significant bias against boys. We heard comments like "because they're stronger"; "they're more active"; "boys have more social and emotional issues than girls"; "boys' vocabulary and hearing isn't as good as girls' "; "boys are more aggressive, hyper, . . . challenging"; and one teacher explicitly stated, "African American boys and men are very unruly and unstable." As in the broader U.S. culture, gender stereotypes abound, and it is relatively easy to find teachers who attest that boys and girls behave differently in the classroom and who demonstrate gender biases toward girls either overtly, as in these interviews, or implicitly in their interactions.

Schools play a significant role in gender stereotyping. As one teacher shared during our interviews, she was very conscious of her differential treatment of boys and girls, and it concerned her. She described catching herself talking differently to boys and girls—always rushing boys from one activity to another and encouraging their gross motor activity ("Come on! . . . Jump! . . . Hurry up!") but she spoke more slowly to girls in her classroom and allowed them more time to transition from one activity to another. She remarked, "It's almost like, here's a child who needs to be settled down and rather than talk quietly and settle him down, we're trying to wear him out, 'let's take him to the park and run his legs off'. . . . Whereas she gets coloring books and purses full of princess stuff to play quietly with." Across numerous studies using teacher reports of children's behavior, boys have been described as more active, more physically aggressive, and slower to achieve academically in areas such as reading. On graphs of children's scores across a variety of characteristics, however, the distributions for boys' and girls' performance overlap (Bigler et al., 2013). There is as much, if not more, variability within each gender as there is a difference between genders. Said another way, you are likely to find similar, if not greater, differences on most psychological traits between two random girls as you are between a boy and a girl.

In response to concerns that the use of teachers' reports of children's behavior introduced too much bias, more recent studies, such as that by Dr. Caroline Bouchard and colleagues in 2015, have triangulated data sources, allowing for the comparison of subjective and objective assessments. By collecting both teachers' reports of children's classroom behavior and directly observing and assessing the social skills of boys and girls, these researchers identified consistent pervasive biases against boys. Preschool teachers in this study rated girls as significantly more prosocial than boys, meaning they perceived girls as more frequently sharing, getting along with others, collaborating, helping peers, and attending to other children's emotions. However, in a structured play observation where all participating children were provided the same materials and opportunities to play with a peer of their choosing, researchers observed no difference between boys' and girls' behaviors. This study focused on positive and prosocial behaviors (as opposed to explicit dangerous or aggressive ones), but it aligns with other studies that have shown that teachers may be less likely to look for and be aware of some children's competencies, in part based on gender. As the adage says, the squeaky wheel gets the grease, and in the classroom, it is no different. Indeed, Arbeau and Coplan (2007) reported that kindergarten teachers spend significantly more time working with and attending to children who present disruptive behaviors, which in turn renders teachers less able to assess other children's behavior accurately.

Perceptions of child gender also drive attributions of emotional causes of behavior. When presented with images of an ambiguously gendered child throwing snowballs, Condry and Ross (1985) found that observers who were told that the child was a boy tended to label the child as feeling angry and displaying aggression. Conversely, when observers were told that the child was a girl, they described her as feeling fearful and her behavior as not aggressive. This experiment demonstrates how gender labels may bias perceptions of the same behavior, which in turn will dictate adults' responses to children's behavior. More recent research in elementary school settings suggests that teachers' gendered perceptions of boys in the classroom may influence teachers' behavior expectancy of the child and further lead the teacher to focus on otherwise normal classroom disruptions and challenging behaviors (Auwarter & Aruguete, 2008; Glock & Kleen, 2017). These perceptions may, in part, explain why boys are much more likely to be referred to special education programs. For decades, the U.S. Office for Civil Rights has reported that among children with severe emotional needs, the male-to-female ratio has remained steady, at about 3.5 boys for every 1 girl (Coutinho & Oswald, 2005).

These pervasive and biased perceptions of boys' abilities—especially around behavioral control—can have significant short- and long-term implications. Teachers' perceptions and expectations of their students influence the quality of their interactions and relationships. Teachers tend to give more attention to boys as compared to girls—both positive and negative—but the quality of the feedback also differs. Boys tend to receive positive verbal feedback more often when behaving or demonstrating academic success and tend to receive more immediate negative feedback for unwanted behavior and classroom disruptions (McLowry et al., 2013). As in the hypothetical example above, a boy running through the classroom is immediately culpable and reprimanded, whereas a girl's motivation for running is considered in a positive light, and she is allowed, if not encouraged, to display her exuberance. Taken together, these biased perceptions against boys' behavior, emotions, and motivations shed light on how rates of exclusionary discipline become so disproportionate.

Importantly, teachers are not alone in their gender-based decision-making, of course. In a study of gender differences in the types of child care parents select for their children, my colleague at the University of Illinois at Chicago, Rachel Gordon, led a team that identified significant parental differences in the perception of and enrollment in care types by child gender (Gordon et al., 2020). Specifically, among lower-income families of boys, parents reported perceiving center-based early childhood programs as less nurturing and safe compared to home-based programs. The opposite was true for girls. Although not directly a study of exclusionary discipline, it is possible that these families were making child-care choices based on the anticipation of biased perceptions of boys' behavior by teachers in center-based care. As we will see in subsequent chapters, although there are limited data on exclusion rates from home-based settings, there is some evidence of lower rates in these contexts.

The impacts of racial biases can and do seep into every aspect of education. As was vibrantly documented in the mini-series *America to Me*, directed by Steve James, biased perceptions of and expectations for Black children—even in a self-proclaimed progressive community—deprive children of color not only of opportunities to be sufficiently challenged in advanced courses, but also of second chances when they make mistakes. The stories depicted in the mini-series align with the results of carefully designed experiments of teachers' decision-making. For example, in one study, English teachers were asked to grade poorly written essays that were randomly assigned stereotypically White, Black, or Latinx names. The papers of children of color were graded significantly more generously. In contrast, White students' papers were held to a higher standard and were assigned lower grades, implying that teachers may hold biased expectations against Black and Latinx students and see them as less capable.

Beyond grading a single assignment, these differential expectations based on race have been linked to the disproportionate rates of Black children being referred for special education services at all grades, and as we have already discussed, higher referrals for disciplinary action (Tenenbaum & Ruck, 2007). Teachers' racially biased expectations contribute to not only their biased decision-making about students of color, but also their behavior toward and interactions with children of color.

Half a century of social psychological research into stereotyping has shown that people rely on stereotypes more—the effects of race on social perception are most substantial—when information is ambiguous. People unconsciously fill in gaps in their understanding and perception and make inferences based on stereotypes. This is why, in part, we see disciplinary disparities are most stark for offenses that rely on subjective interpretations. White children are more likely to be referred to the office in K–12 schools for objectively defined misbehavior, such as smoking or defacing property, whereas Black children are more likely to be referred for a subjective interpretation of their behavior, such as being "threatening." This perception is consistent with the application of racial stereotypes about Black people—especially Black boys—as dangerous or aggressive. When Black children are then punished for a subjective offense, the association is strengthened, and the action is justified—*he must have been threatening and dangerous if he got suspended. The administration agreed with me, and I was right to refer him to the office.* Over time, these reinforced biases can become a self-fulfilling prophecy, with individuals looking for misbehavior more among those who are stereotyped to be more disruptive and dangerous.

Teachers' biased attention to young children's behavior was confirmed in a study by Walter Gilliam and colleagues in 2016 that further connected teachers' unequal attention to children's behavior to preschool disciplinary decision-making. In this study, preschool teachers were invited to watch a series of video clips of four children playing with Play-Doh at a table. They were told the purpose of the study was to understand how teachers detect challenging behavior in the classroom and were asked to push a key on a keyboard every time they saw behavior that could become a potential challenge. While they watched the video, a camera was simultaneously detecting where the participating teachers were looking on the screen. This eye-tracking technology allowed the researchers to measure the amount of times teachers spent looking at each child and which child they were looking at when they clicked the button to report a potential challenge. Importantly, the four children—a White boy, a White girl, a Black boy, and a Black girl—were all well behaved (remained seated, shared materials, etc.) and there were no instances of conflict or misbehavior in the video, so any rating by the teacher was their subjective perception. Results indicated that teachers spent more time closely observing the behavior of Black children, and Black boys in particular, when they were primed to expect challenging behavior to occur. These results mirror the responses teachers provided when asking which child required the most of their attention. The majority of teachers (42%) said that the Black boy required most of their attention. By comparison, only 34% of teachers said they paid the most attention to the White boy. Much smaller proportions of teachers (10% and 13%, respectively) attended most to the White girl and Black girl. If teacher attention were impartial, we would expect that equal proportions of teachers would have indicated watching each child the most. Teachers in this study were self-aware of their enhanced attention to boys broadly, and Black boys in particular, and the objective eye-tracking measurements confirmed this attentional bias. The authors argue that this attentional bias predisposes teachers to see more challenging behaviors among Black boys. In a classroom, it would be easy to see how this plays out. Teachers strategically position themselves around the classroom to be near and responsive to children that will likely need help. You can see this frequently during circle time, when an assistant teacher may sit on the carpet right next to or behind a child who typically struggles to regulate their bodies during a book reading. Children are sometimes asked to move closer to a teacher when they get wiggly. In many ways, this is an advisable practice and helps teachers to be responsive and supportive—two characteristics at the core of high-quality early childhood practice. However, viewed through a different lens, this proactive responsiveness could serve to create a tunnel-vision problem for teachers. To the extent that teachers expect Black children to misbehave and struggle behaviorally, they will pay closer attention to and position themselves to be able to better observe and intervene with these Black children. You cannot see what you do not look for, and this tunnel vision could, in part, explain the well-documented gender and race disparities in preschool expulsions and suspensions.

It is also essential to consider how teachers' racial identities influence their perceptual biases in the classroom. While on average, the early childhood workforce is more racially and ethnically diverse than the K–12 workforce, that diversity is concentrated in assistant and para-professional roles, who have less disciplinary decision-making power (not to mention lower pay;

National Academy of Medicine Report, 2015). Across a multitude of studies, we have seen that Black children are treated differently by their Black and White teachers, but it is not a simple directional difference. Results from a study of nearly 25,000 middle schoolers indicate that when Black children have Black teachers, they are rated as less disruptive and are suspended less often than when they have teachers of another race (Dee, 2005). At the same time, in Gilliam's eye-tracking study, Black teachers spent more time looking at the Black boy in the video and spent less time looking at any other children, compared to White teachers. When these same teachers read vignettes about children misbehaving in the classroom as part of a second study, Gilliam found that Black teachers were more likely to recommend harsher disciplinary actions for Black boys than their White counterparts, indicating that they held Black children to a higher standard of behavior, resulting in a more negative evaluation of their behavior.

Longitudinal work has also demonstrated how Black and White teachers' perceptions of children of color differ over time. Jason Downer and researchers at the University of Virginia examined data representing over 700 state-funded prekindergarten classrooms in 11 states. They found that White teachers reported a more significant increase in Black children's behavior problems from fall to spring, compared to reports by Black teachers. Conversely, when Black children's behavior does not improve in the eyes of White teachers, other research indicates that White teachers tend to escalate their disciplinary responses (Okonofua & Eberhardt, 2015). Downer and colleagues posit that Black teachers may be better equipped to build relationships with and understand the needs of Black children and may also implement a more culturally aligned pedagogy.

In light of all of this evidence, it is clear that American preschools are choked with the same "smog of racism" that Beverly Tatum described in high schools nearly 20 years ago. Ample evidence makes it clear that we cannot pretend that our youngest learners are somehow immune from the adverse effects of implicit biases and overt racism. Further, this smog negatively affects all children, not just children of color. Biased interactions and policies that label subjective behavior as more challenging create a more hostile environment for everyone, regardless of race. The impacts also seep beyond the school walls, as was recently demonstrated in a study by Travis Riddle and Stacey Sinclair (2019). Their paper, published in the *Proceedings of the National Academy of Sciences*, shows that disparities in school-based discipline by race are associated with county-level rates of bias.

Leaving "Colorblind" Mentalities in the Past

Individuals can hold unconscious negative associations against Black children and treat them differently while simultaneously explicitly and vocally disapproving racist attitudes. One example of this tension is in the phenomena of "colorblindness." Colorblind ideology, or the belief that one does not and should not acknowledge race, is common across the field of education. The vast majority of teachers, just like the majority of the U.S. population, do not hold explicit racial biases and want to be effective educators for all of their students. At the same time, many believe that race should not play a factor in their relationship with children. As such, many well-meaning teachers report that they "treat all children the same," "color does not matter," or "I love all of my children equally." As has been well documented elsewhere (and especially by scholars of color, such as Drs. Marisha Humphreys, Stephanie Curenton, Gloria Boutte, and Iheoma Iruka who penned this book's Afterword), equality and equity are not the same, and colorblindness, relegating a significant component of one's identity as unimportant or irrelevant, is itself a racist act.

Despite this desire for equity, many teachers unknowingly hold racial or cultural biases, which interfere with their assessments of classroom situations and individual children's actions, their decision-making, and their relationships, and ultimately compromise the effectiveness of their teaching. Teachers' silence on topics of race not only invalidate the identity, history, and cultural heritage of children of color, but it does not accomplish their goal of equity because it does not prevent children from noting race or developing prejudices of their own. Despite many adults' belief that issues of race are too adult for young children, children are aware of race and the differential treatment of people based on skin color from a very early age, and efforts to "protect" children from adult topics often unintentionally exacerbate racial oppression. To borrow the phrasing of the public health leader Dr. Camara Phyllis during her 2018 keynote address to Early Childhood Leadership fellows at the Erikson Institute, "racism, not race, is a risk factor for expulsion."

To counteract the pervasive bias and dominant culture narratives in early childhood education, anti-bias curricula and trainings and guidance on and assessments of (e.g., Curenton et al., 2020) anti-racist teaching practices have become more prevalent, but still lag far behind what is needed. We will revisit this topic throughout the book, including discussing the importance of cultural competence and humility in developing positive teacher-family relationships (Chapter 7), and the promotion of equity through professional development and coaching (Chapter 8). The Afterword by anti-bias expert Dr. Iheoma Iruka further amplifies the critical role that early childhood education can play in combating racism and inequality, but readers who are interested in a deeper dive on this topic would do well to read her book *Don't Look Away: Embracing Anti-Bias Classrooms* (Iruka et al., 2020).

* * *

Although gender and race are the most prominent and well-studied aspects of bias associated with school discipline, it is important to consider how these factors intersect with one another. A third characteristic has been identified as attracting biased adult attention—size. That is, children may be disciplined more for appearing bigger, and developmentally inappropriate expectations for children's behavior may be due, in part, to misperceptions of children's age. When a child appears ahead of their peers in one aspect of development—for example, height—we may falsely assume they are older or more capable across the board. Taller children are expected to have better expressive and receptive language skills and to be more coordinated or less clumsy. Likewise, children we perceive as older are held to higher standards with regard to their social and emotional skills.

When my son started in home-based child care at the age of 18 months, he was comparatively small—hovering around the 5th percentile for height and weight, according to his pediatrician. The only other child in care at that home was about 6 months older but was in the 98th percentile for height and looked comparatively like a giant. While my son was stumbling as a new walker and still went downstairs backward on his belly, 2-year-old Nelson (pseudonym) was tall enough to climb into his high chair, walked downstairs with ease, and helped himself to items on the kitchen counter. Despite knowing exactly when his birthday was, I perceived him as much older—closer to 3 years old—and evaluated all of his other abilities through this inaccurate lens. His tantrums at drop-off seemed like possible signs of difficulty with transitions, his reliance on pointing and simple two-word phrases could indicate a speech delay, his occasional biting and hitting maybe marked some emotion-regulation challenges. In reality, however, these behaviors are all fully expected and appropriate for a new 2-year-old. All this is to say, even having a Ph.D. in developmental psychology does not render one immune to holding biased expectations for children's behavior based on perceived age (or, unfortunately, many other things). My misperceptions were involuntary and unconscious, and it took active cognitive effort on my part to alter my thinking. If I had been in a position to make decisions about Nelson's care while holding these inappropriate expectations, my rash judgments of his behavior could have had negative implications. Unfortunately, our perception of age does not occur in a vacuum and is itself susceptible to other forms of bias. From the very beginning of a child's educational journey, when Black children walk into the classroom, their predominantly White teachers view them as older than their White peers, creating developmentally inappropriate expectations for behavior (Dancy, 2014).

Perceived age also plays a significant implication in our presumption of innocence or guilt. In a series of experiments published in 2014, social psychologist Phillip Goff and colleagues (Goff et al., 2014) demonstrated that the intersection of biases exacerbates the likelihood that a Black boy will be perceived more as a culpable adult and less as an innocent child compared to same-aged peers. With a sample that reflected the U.S. teaching workforce (that is mostly White and 90% female), the researchers manipulated the age, race, and the severity of the child's behavior. Across the five experiments, participants were asked to rate how old, innocent, and deserving of protection they perceived the children to be. Relevant to this discussion, Goff and colleagues demonstrated that not only are Black boys perceived as less innocent and more responsible for their actions than White children overall, they are also perceived as older than same-aged White and Latino peers.

Further, when a child was described as committing a dangerous act, they were perceived as older than when the behavior was less dangerous. The misperception of age is particularly stark and consequential as children in this study entered early adolescence. Black boys in this study were viewed, on average, to be four and a half years older than they were. As the authors point out, this would mean that 13-year-olds would be misperceived as legal adults and punished accordingly by our criminal justice system. As I demonstrated in the experience with my son above, among younger children, even the misperception of age by 6 months can have significant implications for the way we treat and respond to children. For Black boys, in particular, there is a significant risk of being perceived as bigger and older. Combined with the findings from Gilliam's eye-tracking study, we can see how teachers are highly likely to disproportionately be watching boys who are Black, waiting for them to misbehave, and then perceiving them as less innocent, more culpable, and more deserving of punishment than their White or female peers.

Looking at the reactions of adults in Kaia's story, it is evident that many perceived her as dangerous, volatile, and deserving of significant punishment. However, not all adults responded in the same way. In particular, one teacher saw Kaia as the young child that she is, provided her with the emotional support that she needed in that instance, and helped to de-escalate the situation, albeit temporarily. While it is true that many children, especially Black boys, are subjected to frequent and damaging adult biases—biases that underestimate their cognitive, emotional, and behavioral capabilities—some teachers buck this trend and can more authentically see children for who they are and treat them accordingly. As we have seen above, one possible explanation of teachers' differential treatment of children of color is their own race. Calls for a more representative and diverse teacher workforce are critical, but this alone is not a panacea for exclusionary discipline. Compared to that of K–12, the early childhood workforce is rich in diversity, with a majority of providers being women of color. If the solution of disproportionate discipline was teacher diversity, we should see fewer Black children expelled from preschool classrooms nationwide. Instead, preschool expulsion rates are significantly higher than those in K–12. This disconnect implies that underlying factors may need to be addressed to get at the root of the problem. Beyond teacher identity, it is crucial to consider the contexts in which teachers are making these judgments about children's behavior. Later, we will examine how aspects of the environment—the program and community in which teachers teach—impact discipline practices, but first, we will look inward at the connections between teachers' psychological health and well-being and the exclusion of children from care.

5

Teacher Well-Being and Exclusionary Decision-Making

At the same time that the staff and administrators of Rainbow Bridge were struggling to transition Elijah into another program, they were facing several other challenges in the preschool classroom. In the spring of 2019, two veteran teachers retired. They had worked as co-lead teachers in the preschool-aged Blue room for nearly 15 years. The program director, Ms. Elena, knew their departure was going to leave a void—both logistically and psychologically—so she had planned ahead. Two younger but still experienced teachers had received extra training that year and had been given time to observe and prepare to transition into that classroom. But they were a new teaching pair and did not yet know how to work as a team. In addition to changes in the staff, the kids in the Blue room changed over the summer too, and Ms. Elena hoped that returning kids, like Elijah and Jace (pseudonym), would help the new teachers find their groove come the fall. The Blue room was staffed by two full-time co-lead teachers and a full-time assistant. Together they worked with 18 children, putting the program well below the state's maximum ratio of 1 teacher per 10 children. Children whose birthdays fell after the district's cut-off for kindergarten entry spent two consecutive years in the Blue room, enabling them to serve as knowledgeable leaders and classroom helpers the second go-around, a coveted badge of autonomy at this age group.

In the fall of 2019, however, Jace and Elijah were the only boys returning to the Blue room. In the prior year, Jace had been part of a close-knit group of boys. Like him, they were all from the suburb north of Chicago, into superheroes and building big towers out of blocks. They were also all from low-income Black families, attending Rainbow Bridge with financial assistance through the state's child-care subsidy program. But the others turned five in the preceding months, leaving Jace alone come September.

Ms. Elena had hoped that Jace, a bright boy who was well-liked by the now-retired teachers, could help his new peers and teachers transition into the school year. Soon after the start of the year, however, reports from the Blue room teachers led Ms. Elena to realize that something was different. Jace's behavior was becoming volatile. In staff meetings, the teachers were describing a little boy who was suddenly struggling to control his body and his emotions—throwing materials, screaming wildly, climbing on and knocking over furniture. No one had been harmed, but the teachers were not sure how to help him and worried he would hurt himself. Ms. Elena's best guess was that it was throwing him off not to have those older boys in his class. In hindsight, she could see how they had likely been keeping Jace's behavior in check. In order to be included in their play, Jace had had to act older and more in control of his emotions. Without that social pressure, he was much less inhibited. She was wondering, though, what else could be triggering this dramatic change in his behavior. Then in passing, one of the Blue room teachers mentioned that Jace's father had been the one to do drop-off on Monday. As far as the school knew, Jace's father had not been in his life since birth, so Elena encouraged the teachers to find out more, but without an existing personal relationship, they felt awkward asking for intimate details about arrangements at home. Throughout September, Jace's dad became a fixture of Monday morning drop-offs, as did Jace's struggles to transition into the school week. Hoping that Jace would settle into the new year with a little more time, Elena encouraged the teachers to observe and document Jace's outbursts and try to understand what was going on for him. In October, they finally learned that Jace's parents had gotten back together over the summer, and since the start of the year, Jace had been spending weekends with his father in Wisconsin. Elena and the teachers began to formulate a hypothesis that the frequent family transitions—back and forth from mom to dad—were also making school-day transitions, from lunch to the playground or story time to nap time—incredibly distressing for Jace.

"Saying no to him would lead to complete outbursts," one teacher described, explaining how Jace would react to being redirected by "trashing the classroom." Routinely, Jace would run screaming around the room, tearing baskets of materials off shelves, throwing art supplies and wooden blocks, and climbing on and knocking over shelving. "He's angry and screaming and pushing. The other children are afraid of him. Honestly, I'm afraid of him sometimes." When teachers tried to hold Jace, for example, to take him down from a dangerous position on top of a bookshelf, he would fight back—hitting, biting, kicking, and spitting on the teaching staff. Multiple times a week, episodes like this were derailing the classroom, and it was taking a toll on staff program-wide. "He was the kind of child who would just suck you dry," Ms. Elena recounted. She worried about the amount of time and attention she, her assistant administrator,

and the teachers were spending trying to understand and prevent the outbursts, with no real answers.

Ms. Elena worried about Jace, but she was also profoundly concerned she was about to lose control of the whole situation. Other parents were complaining to the teachers, the teachers were crying in her office after work, and Elena was running out of ideas. She knew they were at a breaking point when one of the new co-lead teachers reacted very poorly to one of Jace's outbursts. "She just lost it with him. Literally had him pinned on the ground. Her co-teacher found her holding him on the ground, trying to restrain him during an outburst." Elena fired the teacher on the spot. She knew she had to, but in the pit of her stomach Ms. Elena knew any of her teachers could have done that—and what's more, she knew it would take her months to find an experienced, well-qualified teacher to fill the vacancy. In the meantime, her other teachers would have to pick up the slack, putting them all under even more pressure.

Following that incident, Elena called for a meeting with Jace's parents, the teachers, and their teaching coach: "it was clear that he wanted and needed more from us, but we were drained." She recommended that Jace move to the nearby school district special education preschool program. Her rationale was that Jace might perceive this as going to the big school and following his older friends who had already started kindergarten. There, the classes were smaller, and there was more one-on-one attention and support. Jace's mother agreed to go with the center's coordinator to tour the program, but on the appointed day, she did not show up. Another date was arranged, and again the mother did not attend. After this second missed appointment, Elena put a letter home in Jace's cubby, reiterating her desire to help them find a more suitable care arrangement for Jace. When Jace was unexpectedly absent for several more days, she emailed the letter home to mom. The next day, Elena received a voicemail from Jace's mother saying they had decided to take him somewhere else. Elena soon heard through her network of local administrators that Jace ended up at a center that is part of a for-profit franchise. She was disappointed and frustrated—not just because Jace's mother had told the new program that Learning Bridge had kicked him out, but because Elena knew that the new program was even less equipped to help him, and the abrupt transition would likely serve to re-trigger so many of Jace's behaviors. Elena reflected on her and her teachers' actions and efforts with a mix of guilt and relief, saying, "Honestly, I am just heartbroken for that little boy."

***

Given that expulsion is an adult decision, we must shift our focus away from factors correlated with being expelled and attend to who the decision-makers are and in what contexts they are making the decision to exclude children. Early childhood educators bear great responsibility and loom large in the lives of young children. The significance, complexity, and emotionality of their work has been routinely reinforced by research. Developmental and educational psychology studies also emphasize the importance of consistency and continuity of caring relationships in the early years. And yet, it is during the first 5 years of life that children in the United States are most likely to interact with a system of care that is fragmented, rife with inconsistencies, and staffed by a workforce that is inadequately supported, provided with few resources, and exploited by low wages. The state of the early childhood workforce has been well reviewed and railed against elsewhere (for example, see the report by the National Research Council, 2015) and was drawn into sharp relief by the recent COVID-19 pandemic when child-care workers were treated as both essential and expendable. This text cannot possibly tackle the entirety of the failings of our nation to support and value our early childhood workforce adequately. Nor do I wish to lay blame on our providers for the exclusion of young children. Instead, in this chapter, I aim to help readers recognize the impossible position in which we often place providers—torn between meeting the needs of an entire classroom and being present with a child struggling emotionally; forced to choose between their own physical and emotional health and safety and the retention of a single child; expected to function in a system that routinely discounts their value despite decades of evidence to the contrary.

The decision to expel a child is not made lightly. Teachers waffle and delay such a decision as long as possible. They are resourceful, creative, persistent, and deeply empathic. At the same time, they are also human, and at some point, they face a seemingly untenable situation, and, feeling hopeless, many make a practical choice. To me, the exclusion of a child is indicative of a teacher at the end of their rope—a teacher so emotionally or physically exhausted that they must triage how they expend their limited remaining energy. They are forced to decide between persisting with an individual child or remaining well enough to work with the other children in their care. This is not to imply that expulsion is a clean break. Grief and remorse linger in the classroom and follow teachers home. However, there is clearly a subset of teachers for whom the strain of working with some children, especially those who pose a challenge behaviorally and emotionally, pushes them to a tipping point. The experience is not ubiquitous. Not every teacher experiences teaching as stressful, or children's behavior as overwhelming, and this variability is borne out in rates of expulsion.

In our study of Chicago area preschool teachers, less than a third of teachers had requested that a child in their classroom be expelled in the prior year, but a smaller proportion, about 10% of all participants, had asked that three or more children be removed in the prior year. A similar trend is seen among teachers of older students. One study found that two-thirds of all disciplinary referrals in one middle school came from less than a quarter of the teachers (Skiba et al., 1997). Teachers may vary in their thresholds of tolerance for misbehavior or have different definitions for what constitutes "removable" behavior. These intrapersonal factors are sensitive to teachers' other experiences, thoughts, and actions across settings. In particular, teachers' ability to support children's social and emotional behavior in the classroom is tied to their own well-being. In this chapter, after a broad overview of sources of teachers' stress and distress in early childhood education, we will begin to consider the role that teachers' emotional well-being (including their experiences of stress, depression, and sense of self-efficacy) play in the decision to exclude children. We will examine how teachers' negative perceptions of children and families, and subsequently their requests for expulsion, are tied to their feelings at work.

Why Are Teachers Crying at Work?

Teaching, especially in early childhood, has long been described as a highly rewarding occupation (Bloom, 1986; Thomason & La Paro, 2013), but it is also described as emotionally challenging (e.g., Johnson et al., 2005). Early childhood educators report experiencing more stress and being less physically healthy than their non-teaching peers (Whitaker et al., 2013). Although they consistently indicate that children's challenging behaviors (defiance, aggression, etc.) detract from their well-being at work (Hoover et al., 2012), there are a host of other root causes for early childhood teachers' distress.

One of the most commonly cited reasons for early childhood educators' poor physical and emotional health is their inadequate compensation and the lack of pay parity with other educators. In comparison to the general population, early childhood education teachers are among the most economically insecure workers in the United States (Phillips et al., 2016). A 2016 report by the U.S. Departments of Education and Health and Human Services highlighted that the national median annual wage for center-based preschool teachers hovered just above the federal poverty line for a family of four ($28,570 respectively). In child care, wages are even lower, closer to $20,000 a year, on average. Parity across delivery systems is also abysmal. Preschool teachers working in school-based preschool programs make nearly twice as much as their community-based peers, and those serving children just a few months older in kindergarten earn, on average, $51,640 per year, in addition to receiving full benefits. Nationally, nearly half of early childhood educators depend on some form of public assistance, and only 15% receive employer-sponsored health insurance. It should be no surprise, therefore, that early childhood teachers quit. Average turnover across surveyed Illinois programs in 2017 was 37%, and many programs reported rates over 100%. This disruption first became tangible for me in graduate school when the entire staff at a center where I was collecting data turned over in the course of a school year; by May, everyone from the director to the classroom aides was brand new. While it was mildly annoying to have to re-explain the study nearly 25 times, the children and families were especially impacted by the revolving door of staff. High turnover is both a cause and result of stressful working conditions and teacher burnout. Worse yet, it undermines the relationship-based nature of early education and sows inconsistency, which can wreak havoc for children and families.

Pay is not the only source of stress and dissatisfaction at work. Early childhood educators must keep children physically safe and emotionally secure, provide instruction to meet various learning standards and expectations, and communicate effectively with families and co-workers—tasks that are exponentially harder when working with children who exhibit behavioral and emotional difficulties. Further, teachers are increasingly expected to meet accountability demands—conducting assessments, generating detailed lesson plans and documentation, and engaging in professional development activities. Despite all of these demands, teachers also have little control or autonomy in their classrooms. Because of mandated teacher-child ratios, work hours are highly structured, and teachers cannot easily take breaks or step out of the classroom momentarily. Likewise, teachers have little control over whom they are partnered with for co-teaching and have few opportunities for discretion, such as experimenting with new teaching techniques. As in the broader population, teachers vary in their perception of these job demands and the extent to which they experience their workplaces as stressful, but the high turnover rates are indicative of a generally strained system.

Beyond workplace stress, research has underscored the role that teachers' backgrounds, experiences, and home lives play in their emotional health and well-being. Early childhood educators are often of and from the communities in which they teach. Although this can lead to greater cultural competence and shared identities with children and families, it also means that many teachers experience the same concentrated poverty and have experienced similar adversities to the children we described in Chapter 3. In their 2020 paper published in *Children and Youths Services Review*, Dr. Grace Hubel and colleagues found that teachers from participating child-care centers experienced, on average, more childhood adversities (ACEs) than the general population (Hubel et al., 2020). Nearly three-quarters of teachers had experienced at least one, and almost a quarter had experienced four or more ACEs. By comparison, data from the Centers for Disease Control reported by Merrik and colleagues in 2018 show that 62% of the general U.S. population has experienced one ACE, and only 16% experienced four or more ACEs. Child-care teachers participating in this study experienced high rates of significant adversity.

In addition to many growing up with divorced parents, 43.1% of early childhood educators had experienced childhood emotional abuse. One in four were physically abused or lived with an adult with a substance abuse problem. Approximately one in five teachers reported that they had lived with an adult who experienced mental health problems (21.6%), had witnessed domestic violence (21.5%), or had been sexually abused as a child (19.8%). Finally, 11.1% of the sample reported that they had lived with an adult who was incarcerated during their childhood. Beyond describing these distressing levels of adversity among early childhood education teachers, this study also demonstrated that teachers with higher ACE scores tended to have larger classes. The correlation between experiencing physical abuse in childhood and teaching a larger number of students was significant and positive. Other studies have shown that children are more likely to be expelled from larger classrooms. Even controlling for the effect of class size, the Hubel study went further by observing classroom environments, and found that teachers who reported a higher number of ACEs taught in classrooms with poorer social-emotional climates. Teachers who had an incarcerated parent or experienced childhood physical or emotional abuse in particular struggled to create a classroom environment that could positively foster children's emerging social and emotional skills. As the authors speculate in their discussion, experiencing these ACEs, in particular, is indicative of teachers not being exposed to parental models of sensitive and responsive caregivers in their own formative years. In fact, with regard to the last two significant ACEs, these teachers likely were exposed to high levels of harsh, insensitive, and punitive parenting. Other studies have reported similarly high levels of ACEs among other child welfare professionals (e.g., Esaki & Larkin, 2013; Howard et al., 2015), and early childhood teachers may be motivated to enter the workforce because they are empathic to the needs of children who face adversity.

At the same time, prior research into ACEs and toxic stress have demonstrated that these early experiences can have detrimental impacts on neurological functioning. Adults who have higher ACE scores have been shown to struggle to regulate their emotions, cope with stress, and build relationships. When in the classroom, therefore, teachers who have themselves experienced more considerable adversity, especially in the form of insensitive or absent caregiving, are emotionally ill-equipped to care professionally for children. Without sufficient training and support, therefore, the very same adversities that are associated with being expelled may also be associated with being a teacher who ultimately expels children in their care. Regardless of the sources of stress—whether rooted in early adversity, an outcome of persistent economic disadvantage, or the result of restrictive working conditions, any discussion of reforming early childhood discipline practices and reducing reliance on exclusion must attend to the emotional health and well-being of teachers.

Early childhood teachers' experiences of stress negatively impact their work with children. Teachers' emotional well-being can influence their relationships with students, classroom management styles, and the quality of their teaching (Jennings & Greenberg, 2009). Some teachers who are overwhelmed or stressed at work may be more fatigued, inattentive, frustrated, or irritable. Especially during challenging times in the classroom, some teachers, but not all, who are already emotionally depleted may struggle to manage their physiological arousal in healthy ways. Others find ways to successfully manage and mitigate experiences of stress so that they do not detract from their relationships with students and co-workers, enabling them to view their work as more enjoyable (Goddard et al., 2004). While broader efforts address the poor working conditions and high stress of the early childhood education workforce, understanding teachers' different responses to strain may provide critical insight into the expulsion process.

We have long known that children living with a parent with major depression or other significant mood disorders can negatively impact young children's social-emotional and cognitive development. Children raised by depressed mothers typically display weaker social skills and higher problem behaviors. Given the attachment-like relationships that children form with their early teachers and child-care providers, it is not surprising that similar associations have been identified among teacher emotional health, instructional quality, classroom climate, teacher-child relationships, emotionally supportive teaching practices, and perceptions of and reactions to challenging behavior. Children in classrooms with emotionally distressed or depressed teachers perform more poorly on some academic assessments and struggle with social skills like cooperation. Preschool teachers who self-report having lower levels of emotional competence, including emotion-regulation skills, tend to have students who perform more poorly on measures of attention regulation and display greater problem behavior (Jennings, 2011). Job-related stress may undermine a teacher's ability to provide consistent and emotionally supportive classroom environments. In one of my first papers using classroom observation data, we observed teachers' reactions to children's emotions and found that those teachers who reported experiencing higher levels of stress in the classroom were consistently less supportive in their responses to children's negative emotions (Zinsser et al., 2013). Stressed or emotionally exhausted teachers on the "burnout cascade" (Jennings & Greenberg, 2009) may be less able to manage the social and emotional challenges in their classroom. This negative feedback loop between teachers and children is not unique to preschool. The mental health of a child's teacher has also been correlated with a widening of the achievement gap in elementary school. Academically at-risk children with depressed teachers make smaller gains in mathematical skills over the school year as compared to similarly at-risk peers with non-depressed teachers (McLean & Connor, 2015). Compared to public school K–12 teachers, however, early childhood educators, including home-care, center-based, and even many school-based teachers, are significantly less likely to make a livable wage, have access to medical and behavioral health benefits, and receive much less guidance and structural support around the management of children's challenging behaviors.

The connection between teachers' well-being and children's classroom experiences have been studied for nearly 40 years. Studies have examined the causal pathways to explain teacher stress (e.g., Tellenback et al., 1983), how teachers cope with stress (e.g., Borg, 1990), how schools can reduce stress (Sheffield et al., 1994), and intervention programs for teachers who are stressed (Roger & Hudson, 1995). However, little of this research has directly tied teacher stress to their utilization of various disciplinary practices. Our first indication that stress was a factor to consider in early childhood expulsion came from Gilliam and Shahar's 2006 study of a mental health consultation intervention in public preschool programs. Although not the primary research question of the study, results indicated that highly stressed teachers are up to three times more likely to expel a child than their less-stressed peers. In that 2006 paper, the authors called for action, saying:

> Regardless of any causal directionality between job stress and expulsion, these two variables appear to be meaningfully related, and mental health service providers should consider the potential utility of direct services to preschool teachers aimed at decreasing feelings of job stress and increasing teachers' feelings regarding the positive impacts they may be having on the children placed in their care. (Gilliam & Shahar, 2006, p. 16)

Despite that earnest call, studies of preschool and early childhood exclusion paid little heed. In our meta-analysis of the expulsion literature, we found only one study published between 2006 and 2019 that assessed teacher emotional health: Upshur et al. (2009) measured whether changes in teachers' emotional exhaustion accounted for teacher-rated improvements in children's behavior scores. The results were insignificant, but given that expulsion was reported at the center level, the study was not able to address the question regarding variation in disciplinary practice directly.

Having worked for several years on other studies of teacher well-being and connections to children's emerging emotional competence, this seemed like a natural gap to fill. With funding from the National Academy of Education and the Spencer Foundation, I designed a study to more directly examine the connections between teachers' experiences of well-being at work and their utilization of exclusionary discipline. Data for this study were collected in the spring of 2016, a dynamic time in the city of Chicago with regard to early childhood disciplinary practice and policy. In the prior school year, Chicago Public Schools (CPS) enacted a new student charter prohibiting the expulsion of children in prekindergarten through 2nd grade. However, these mandates do not apply to the 1,800 center-based programs serving over 11,500 preschool-age children in the Chicago metropolitan area. Therefore, through this study, we aimed to garner a better understanding of the social-emotional and disciplinary experiences of teachers and children in these community center–based child-care and preschool programs.

Collecting field data in Chicago in February is not advisable for the warm-blooded, but my fantastic team of undergraduate and graduate students rose to the challenge and knocked on the doors of nearly 100 child-care centers in 13 purposefully selected neighborhoods throughout Chicago. The resulting sample included responses from teachers working in majority White, Black, and Latino neighborhoods across three median household income bands determined by the U.S. Census. With administrators' blessing, we recruited teachers to complete surveys reporting on their training, workplace experiences, management of challenging behavior, recent requests to have a child expelled, and psychological well-being. On average, responses were received from teachers at 43% of eligible centers in each neighborhood type, and approximately 26% of lead teachers at a given center (based on parallel director staffing reports). In addition to the survey data collected from 127 teachers, an additional 30 teachers were invited to participate in follow-up interviews. These were again purposefully sampled, this time to ensure that the interviewed teachers reflected the full range of expulsion experiences and neighborhood diversity. Twenty-seven teachers (or 90% of those recruited) completed the follow-up interviews via telephone.[1]

Because I was interested in teacher-level decision-making (rather than administrator actions), surveys asked teachers to indicate how often in the prior 12 months they had asked to have a child permanently removed from their classroom because of behavior problems. As was indicated above, expulsion requests were reasonably common, with more than a quarter of the sample requesting that at least one child be removed and 1 in 10 teachers making three or more requests. When asked to describe the child whom they most recently asked to have removed from their classrooms, teachers reported that the majority of these children were 4 years old, male, and Black. Children were asked to leave primarily for displaying unsafe behaviors.

[1] For a fuller methodological description, including the qualitative coding scheme, see Zinsser, K. M., Zulauf, C. A., Das, V. N., & Silver, H. C. (2019), Utilizing social-emotional learning supports to address teacher stress and preschool expulsion, *Journal of Applied Developmental Psychology*, *61*, 33–42.

Teachers requesting expulsions did not significantly differ from those who had not asked to have children removed with regard to age, years of experience, or education level, or neighborhood type,[2] but expulsion requests were slightly more common among teachers in for-profit, as opposed to not-for-profit, centers. Relevant to this discussion, analysis of the survey data confirmed the findings of Gilliam and Shahar's 2006 study: teacher-reported levels of stress and depression were higher among those who had requested expulsions. Further, stress was a significant positive predictor of the number of expulsion requests, even after controlling for their years of experience, the ratio of children-to-teachers in their classrooms, and the number of social-emotional supports and resources they had. While these results were a critical addition to the literature, replicating a concerning association from public prekindergartens in a sample of community-based child-care programs, the qualitative interviews were even more illuminating.

Using survey data, we constructed comparison groups of teachers who had and had not requested at least one expulsion in the prior year. In the follow-up interviews, these groups described their sources of and experiences of stress very differently and also discussed qualitatively different approaches to managing their workplace distress. More than half of the teachers in the non-expulsion group did not mention feelings of stress during the interview. As one teacher described, instead, "In the classroom, I am the calmest that I am throughout the day." When teachers did describe feeling "exhausted" or "drained," they were just as likely to attribute it to high pressure from their program around promoting school readiness and annual classroom evaluations as to child behavior. These acknowledgments of stress were also often accompanied by an awareness of the impact of their emotions on the children. As one said, "Sometimes there are kinds of things and pressures on me that really have nothing to do with my students, that influence how I am feeling and . . . my capacity to kind of roll with the punches weakens just a little bit."

Conversely, among teachers who had expelled at least one child, discussions of experiencing stress were frequent, and stress was consistently referenced throughout the interviews. Further, this group of teachers

[2] In a separate analysis with these same data, we included four dichotomously coded variables for neighborhood income/racial majority in logistic regression models predicting expulsion request (with low income/White being the reference group). Teachers overwhelmingly reflected the racial majority of the neighborhoods in which they taught, so this could be a proxy variable for teacher race. None was a significant predictor of the dichotomous expulsion variable (Silver & Zinsser, 2020).

attributed their stress to specific children. Often, some of this stress arose from having to manage the needs of one child while still attending to the rest of the class. As one teacher described, balancing the needs of specific children contributes to a waning sense of efficacy: "Especially when you've got 17, and there are 5 out of the 17 children that's in the classroom with behavior [problems], the teacher can't teach or educate the children because you are trying one-on-one with the child with the behavior and what happens is you burn out the teacher." These teachers were also the only ones to describe the physical sources of stress in their rooms, such as having to restrain children engaged in dangerous or harmful behaviors. Several teachers also discussed how not being part of a team could also be a source of stress. As one teacher said, "I was at the end of my rope; I did all I could. I mean, I tumbled, I twirled, I was the sole teacher." One teacher expressed increased concern when she was alone because of her inability to protect the other children from witnessing inappropriate behavior. She wished someone else could "remove that child, so the other children don't have to witness that and won't become traumatized from seeing a child lash out at an adult in that manner."

Beyond differences in their experiences and sources of stress, teachers who did and did not request expulsions also approached the management of these negative feelings differently. One teacher from the non-expulsion group described doing a self-assessment when she begins to feel stressed in the classroom, and allowing herself the leniency to rearrange the classroom schedule to make sure that she and the children can stay on an even keel, saying, "I try to analyze what is going on . . . how it affects me, and then if at that time I feel like if they can play more outside rather than teaching or doing any circle time, those kinds of stuff." Two teachers described having to actively remind themselves to take deep breaths during challenging moments. In both instances, these teachers explained that such breaths helped them to remember how much they enjoyed their interactions with these specific children; ". . . this little boy is pushing me over the edge, I take a deep breath and ask him if he needs a hug. I mean, he usually says, 'yes teacher.' I mean, he is a snuggly little guy, and I'll just hold him until he's ready to go on and move on. But I find for me that helps me diffuse my feelings". Similarly, another teacher explained that she was "driving home yesterday and . . . thinking, I've got to remember, take a deep breath, I've got to remember, he's challenging when he's there, but when he does come in, and I'm sitting next to him, a nice, strong, soft side of me comes out."

In contrast, teachers in the expulsion group did not consistently discuss how they managed their stress. The few who did discuss stress management mentioned taking short breaks from the classroom. They described leaving for 5 minutes to go to the bathroom, taking some deep breaths, and drinking some water before going back in. These data provide valuable insight into variations in teachers' approaches to stress management by expulsion tendency. Stressed teachers who recently expelled children described using short breaks from stressful interactions as their primary management strategy. Those who retained children appear to be reflecting on their styles of interaction and cognitively reframing their relationships with individual children in order to regulate their stress. Although taking short breaks may be a viable short-term solution for some teachers, it does not appear to address the underlying root causes of stress for teachers. Unfortunately, when removing oneself from the child is not practical, one of the only options left in these teachers' toolboxes was to manage their stress by permanently removing the child. Reflecting on styles of interaction and cognitively reframing a relationship with a child seems to be a viable long-term solution for teachers.

Although this Chicago-area study did replicate the higher rates of exclusion of boys and children of color, a fundamental limitation was that it did not directly assess how feeling stressed may exacerbate teachers' reliance on biases during expulsion decision-making. However, from other literature, we can see how these three factors—stress, implicit biases, and decision-making—are connected. In *Thinking Fast and Slow*, Daniel Kahneman (2011) describes how decision-making in times of stress can be flawed. Evolutionarily, the ability to rapidly assess a threat was advantageous when our ancestors needed to decide whether to fight or run from a predator. At the same time, when we do things more quickly, we often make mistakes. Shortcuts require reliance on assumed relationships between events or characteristics—a loud sound in the woods must come from something large and scary. These presumed relationships may or may not be accurate. Cognitive psychologists liken implicit biases to these cognitive heuristics—shortcuts our brains rely on to accelerate decision-making. When we make assumptions that center around a group—such as the notion that Black children are more likely to misbehave—the cognitive error can lead to implicit bias toward that group. We saw this phenomenon concretely in the eye-tracking study by Gilliam and colleagues in the prior chapter. Teachers' assumptions about who was most likely to misbehave led them to overwhelmingly narrowly focus their attention on those children. At the same time, there is a rich literature demonstrating how reliance on such heuristics is amplified when an individual is fatigued or stressed. For example, emergency room (ER) doctors score higher on tests of the implicit racial association after working a shift when the ER was overcrowded, and they were carrying a high patient load, compared to scores before their shift or after shifts when the ER was not overcrowded (Johnson et al., 2016). Increased biased decision-making during times of stress can then result in patients of color receiving poorer quality care, such as having their pain be undertreated compared to White patients (Hoffman et al., 2016). The effect of stress has also been examined in relation to the perception of children's behavior. When highly stressed, clinicians working with youth fall back on implicit and explicit biases to make decisions about treatment and diagnosis (Fadus et al., 2020). This is one possible explanation for the higher rates of more severe disorder diagnoses among Black children compared to White peers. Black children who are displaying challenging behavior are disproportionately diagnosed with more severe disorders, such as conduct disorder or oppositional defiant disorder. In contrast, their White peers displaying similar behaviors are diagnosed with attention-deficit/hyperactivity disorder (ADHD), even after controlling for confounding variables such as income and experiences of adversity.

We have nearly four decades of research demonstrating that teachers, especially those in early childhood, are emotionally exhausted, stressed, and depressed. The impacts of teacher mental health on student outcomes are similarly well understood to be negative. What is more, as we saw in Chapter 4, there is similarly no doubt about the cost of implicit biases and racism for young children of color. Early childhood teachers inhabit a unique position in our society. They wield a great deal of power and influence over the trajectory of young children's lives—fostering and facilitating growth and maturation, paving a pathway toward success in school and life. At the same time, they are habitually discounted by the very society that relies so heavily on their labor. Poor pay, limited benefits, insufficient support and resources, and general disrespect have taken a toll on the well-being of our early childhood education providers, many of whom have experienced substantial hardship and adversity early in life. Under stress, teachers' decision-making capabilities are hampered, biases are exacerbated, and children, especially Black children, are pushed out of care. In order to intervene, however, we must better understand exactly how the process of expulsion unfolds.

6

The "How" of Exclusion

When Noel (pseudonym) was born, his mom, Mia (pseudonym), was living alone and worked as an adjunct college professor. Because her position did not come with benefits like maternity leave, Mia was back in the lecture hall soon after Noel was born. The baby spent most days in those early months with a family friend who worked nights. Eventually, Mia found a home-based child care nearby, and for over a year, Noel was doted upon by the caregivers there. When work moved the little family to Pennsylvania, a new home-based program told Mia that Noel was "the easiest child," and everyone was happy at pick-up each day.

In 2017, when Noel was two, Mia accepted a job in South Carolina and set about trying to enroll Noel in a new child-care arrangement before classes started. She immediately noticed how hard it was to find any programs with openings, let alone programs where she was comfortable leaving Noel. "Most of the places I went into, they either smelled like dirty diapers or the girls who worked there looked miserable, and the children looked terrified to make a peep. It was really hard to find a place that I felt reasonably comfortable to leave him. I had to work, of course, and I finally found one that seemed reasonably good—the people seemed nice, the kids seemed happy."

Noel had a honeymoon period for a few weeks. There we no problems, and the teachers reported that he was settling in without any issues. "Then suddenly, [in the 3rd week] he was crying uncontrollably when I would take him there in the morning. They assured me that he would calm down after I left, but soon after I started getting phone calls." Beginning about a month into Mia's new job, the program started calling her several times a week, asking her to come to pick him up early "because he was starting to act out, pushing other children but mostly he was very needy and needed a lot of attention from the teacher, and they were having a hard time handling him." Mia could see the writing on the wall and started getting anxious. "In late September, I voiced some concerns. I said, 'you guys have been calling me a lot to pick him up early, and he has been getting a lot of "write-ups" for scratching other kids and pushing other kids. Are you going to kick him out?' And they said, 'No, as long as he's not biting, we don't expel children, we are just going to try to work with this and see what we can do.'"

A few weeks later, Mia got some additional insight into the program's concerns. At pick-up one day, a teacher mentioned that Noel seemed to get really frustrated when he could not communicate with them. Mia shared that he had had several ear infections when he was very small, so that his eardrum caved in, and he had short-term hearing loss. Mia thought maybe his hearing issues were cropping up again and impacting his communication. At home, she never had trouble understanding him, and he did not get frustrated, but at school, especially with teachers who didn't know him as well, maybe this could be the root of his aggression? She was almost relieved to be able to point the finger at why her sweet, easy little boy was causing so many problems. Although Mia didn't receive benefits, Noel did qualify for Medicaid, so Mia took him to be evaluated. At the appointment in early October, Mia received a mixed report. His vocalizations and expressive and receptive vocabulary were well within developmental expectations for a young 2-year-old. However, the developmental screener at the family medicine practice Mia was referred to also mentioned that Noel might have a sensory processing disorder. "What does that mean?!" Mia asked at the appointment, but beyond a thin pamphlet, she did not get many answers and felt utterly lost about how to proceed.

Not long after Mia shared the results of the evaluation with the program, she was asked to come in early to meet with the director. "I remember it was the day of the Halloween parade, and when I showed up for a meeting with the director, she just said, 'We actually want you to clean out his things, we don't want you to come back. We just can't handle him. He's too aggressive, he's biting, and we don't have the staff to handle his needs.' And that was it. I had to wake him up from nap and take him home."

Mia tried to stay calm as she brought Noel home and settled him in. But when she finally got a moment alone, "I burst into tears. I didn't understand what was going on. He was fine until we moved down here. He never bit anyone before—in fact, he came home with bite marks from other kids, but I didn't make anything of it. Kids bite at this age. It's normal!" She reflected that the "meeting" with the director was the first mention of Noel biting, but maybe that's what the teacher was hinting at when she said he was "frustrated." She looked over the incident reports she had received, and they all recounted Noel pushing other children, mostly on the playground, and always "unprovoked." None of them mentioned biting or the behavior escalating beyond a playground scuffle. She felt blindsided by the expulsion.

Mia's mind was reeling. Was Noel unfairly targeted and labeled as a troublemaker, or was there something seriously wrong? At the same time, she was becoming increasingly anxious about losing her job. As an adjunct professor, she had very little job security and was working on short-term contracts at multiple institutions—driving between campuses to teach large lectures on art history. Mia started calling child-care programs, but many around her were full or too expensive. In the meantime, Noel came to class with her. For a couple of weeks, they were making it work—he would have a stack of coloring books and a bag of snacks and sit in the back row—until one day when her Department Chair came to conduct a surprise teaching observation. That night, in a state of panic about losing her job, Mia signed a contract to enroll Noel in a Montessori program, "The transition was surprisingly smooth." He was in a classroom with just 2-year-olds (unlike the larger mixed-age group at the last program). Over the first few months, they sent a few notes home mentioning incidents with a little bit of pushing and that he would sometimes randomly run off when they wanted him to line up to go somewhere in the building.

As his birthday approached, Noel was transferred to the 3-to-6-year-old group. That's when the problems reappeared. Mia immediately noticed the environmental differences between the classrooms. The new room was larger (24 kids in one room), it was noisier, and, in line with the Montessori method, they expected a lot from the children (i.e., cleaning up their own materials and working independently). A few weeks into the new classroom, she received the first incident report saying that Noel had bitten another child.

To Mia's relief, when the first phone call came, they weren't calling to have Noel picked up early. They were calling to encourage Mia to have him reevaluated. Unlike the prior program, it was evident to Mia that this Montessori program had been "collecting data" and trying to really understand the why, when, and what of Noel's aggression. They had some really concrete examples and had identified some triggers. His teacher reported that she believed that he knew that his behavior was wrong, "they said he would look embarrassed and put his eyes down when they admonished him" and that it normally happened during really active busy times, either outside on the playground or during the transition to lunch when there were noise and movement.

The program highly recommended a specific children's mental health specialist whom they had successfully worked with in the past—she would come to observe children at the program and work directly with the teachers to find solutions. But unfortunately, Medicaid would not cover her services, and Mia was left to find someone else on her own. For a few weeks, she took Noel to a behavioral therapist, but it was clear early on that it wasn't a good fit. Mia was frustrated that it seemed like three-quarters of every session was the therapist admonishing her for not disciplining Noel at home. To Mia, this didn't make any sense—he didn't do these behaviors at home, and why would it be useful to discipline him for misbehavior at school, 5 or 6 hours after the fact? But the real challenge came when the therapist tried to dictate techniques for the teachers to use at school—specifically behavior charts and tokens (e.g., if you don't bite today, then you get 15 minutes of extra free choice time). The Montessori program was adamant that they would not implement a reward-and-punishment system. It was antithetical to their pedagogy. This clash over styles drove a wedge between the therapist and the teachers, leaving Mia, once again, on her own. Mia confronted the therapist, saying that it didn't seem like this approach was working for Noel. He was still biting and pushing; she was still getting phone calls about his behavior, leaving work early, and was very worried about losing her job. Rather than a sympathetic ear, however, the therapist admitted that she didn't really know much about sensory processing disorder and wasn't well-positioned to help Noel after all.

Mia had been upfront with the Montessori about why Noel had left his prior program, and throughout his time there, she felt that the program was also honest and open with her. She felt that there had been good communication with the school—especially with one assistant teacher who would share insights with Mia about what was going on, what seemed to set Noel off, and what worked for her to help calm him down. After the failed attempt with the therapist, the program director invited Mia to meet and discuss other options. "They genuinely wanted to help him, I will say that about the Montessori program, they meant well and wanted to help him, but it was too much for him to be in that big room. He was OK in the smaller ones, but now that he was 3, it was too much. There was too much going on and too much noise." Eventually, the Montessori program began to not-so-subtly hint that Mia needed to find another arrangement for Noel. "He wasn't expelled officially, but it was clear that we weren't really welcome there anymore, even though they wanted to help, they couldn't."

With luck, Mia found another program with an opening right away—a church-based preschool with small classes. "He had a great first week—14 kids, all his same age," but then Hurricane Dorian hit North Carolina, and the school closed for a week. "When we came back, all the old problems started happening again—the kicking, the biting, always after lunch, always on the playground." This program also wanted to work with Mia and find a solution, but they warned that if they couldn't find one, then he would have to go home each day before lunch (11:30 a.m.). Looking at her course schedule with back-to-back classes most afternoons, Mia was desperate to find a solution too. The school recommended that she contact Child Find through the school district—a service that provides screenings and general education interventions—to see if Noel qualified for an individualized education plan (IEP). Mia's numerous phone calls went unreturned, and even the director's attempt to call on her behalf was unsuccessful. Frantic to do "something" to prove to the program that she was trying, she took Noel to the pediatrician in hopes than any evaluation was better than none. Unfortunately for Mia, the appointment further undercut her confidence and hope. "He told me that sensory processing disorder was a hoax and that the problem was 'only child syndrome,' whatever that means." Mia said that the doctor further blamed her for not disciplining him enough. "I was crushed and exhausted. . . . I am terrified of the school calling and jump when my phone rings. I felt ashamed that I'm not a good mother." Subsequent phone calls from the school didn't help. "When I got off the phone with his teacher just the other day, I was fairly convinced that Noel is growing up to be a sociopath—'it was unprovoked,' they said—that he can't possibly grow up to be a productive member of society."

The saga has taken its toll on Mia emotionally and financially too. Although there is no proof, she suspects she has lost out on job opportunities and had her classes cut because this whole situation has eroded her reputation as a professional. "You can only cancel class so many times before the students start talking, and it gets back to the Department Chairs." Mia was even contemplating moving out of state again, back up to New England, because she was worried that both Noel and she were getting a bad reputation in South Carolina. "He's getting noticed as a bad apple, and the teachers are watching him more closely than any other child in the room. If he ever gets evaluated and labeled with an IEP, will he ever escape that bias against him?" What gnaws at Mia, too, is that she has never personally witnessed the behaviors the teachers report. She does not doubt them necessarily, she just cannot fathom it. "He's the sweetest kid. He's so gentle with pets and loves sea animals. He loves them so much that he refuses to eat fish. When we go to the library or community center, he always plays nicely with others and sits quietly at story time."

***

It is clear from Noel's story that programs vary widely in how they approach exclusions. For some, it is an efficient business decision, made with little preamble or communication with the family. For others, it is the end of a long, drawn-out process for experimentation and adaptation. Understanding variations in and similarities across these processes may be an essential step toward devising policies and interventions to curtail exclusion. Unfortunately, although we know a fair amount about who is expelled and why they are expelled, there has been limited research on where expulsion is most likely and even less on exactly how expulsion happens in early childhood. In our systematic review of the early childhood education expulsion literature (Zinsser et al., 2022), only 5 of the 20 studies assessed whether programmatic characteristics such as program type (home-based vs. center-based), funding (public vs. private), or various practices and resources were associated with rates of exclusionary discipline. Unsurprisingly, given the small evidence base, these findings are also often in conflict with one another. In his 2006 study, Gilliam found that teachers who had expelled a child for challenging behavior were most likely to work in for-profit child-care programs. The lowest exclusion rates were in Head Start and school-based programs. Six years later, a team led by Sarah Hoover at the University of Colorado, School of Medicine, reported that rates of removals among Colorado early childhood education programs were significantly higher in family child-care homes (35 per 1,000) than in child care centers (6 per 1,000). Allison Hooper and Claire Schweiker at the University of Alabama, Tuscaloosa, analyzed a nationally representative data set of home-based care providers collected that same year and found that the use of expulsion could be partially explained by the provider and program characteristics. Providers who had at least some college credits (as opposed to a high-school diploma or GED), were White, and were younger were more likely to expel at least one child.

My work replicates and extends some of these findings and contradicts others. Teachers from for-profit programs in my Chicago-area preschool teacher study were more likely to request one or more expulsion than those in nonprofit settings, but education and experience were not associated with requests. In contrast, administrators from publicly funded programs who completed our 2018 survey of Illinois early childhood education administrators reported higher rates of expulsion overall compared to private and for-profit programs (Silver et al., 2021). From this same state-wide study, rates of expulsion were higher in center-based programs as opposed to school- or home-based programs. Rates also tended to be higher in programs that were fully publicly funded as compared to those in which at least some parents paid tuition. Program location and quality mattered, too—programs located in Chicago versus elsewhere in Illinois and those of modest quality expelled more children than high-quality programs. Finally, rates of expulsion also varied by the racial-ethnic makeup of students enrolled in the program. Specifically, diverse programs with no racial/ethnic majority tended to expel more children than programs with a majority racial or ethnic group. This last finding was a partial replication of our findings from the Chicago-area teacher study in which teachers expelled more children and especially more Black children from diverse classrooms than from racially homogeneous ones.

Reading across these studies, it is clear that more work is needed to ascertain a reliable pattern of results. Some of the variability in results is due to differences in measurement. Some studies, such as those by Gilliam and Hoover, used dichotomous indicators of expulsion (e.g., in the past 12 months, did your program expel any child, yes or no?), whereas others queried the number of expulsions in total. Who was reporting likely also played a role. Surveys of teachers focus on requests for or risk of expulsions since they are often not the final determinant of enrollment. Conversely, administrators may have more access to the final exclusionary discipline tallies. Nevertheless, taken together, these studies continue to underscore the idea that context matters. In Chapter 5, we saw that some essential contextual factors are intra-personal. In this chapter, we will expand this assessment to include more distal factors such as programmatic policies and procedures. Mirroring the two approaches to reporting on expulsion rates above, we will first consider the process from the teachers' perspective before attending to the process at the program level and the role of the administrator.

Inside the Classroom Door

We have already discussed at length how teachers differ in their perceptions of a child's behavior and the fact that those perceptions are vulnerable to implicit and explicit biases and heightened by certain conditions such as stress and adversity. It is likewise important to understand how teachers experience the process of expelling a child—from their first report of a problem to their supervisor through the child's departure. As with other topics in this book, there is limited empirical evidence to draw on, but what we do have paints a somewhat bleak picture.

Researchers Karin Martin, Emily Bosk, and Denise Bailey conducted a series of in-depth qualitative interviews with child-care providers to explore how teachers experience the expulsion process. The results of this analysis were published in a 2018 issue of *Children & Society* and provide the first working model to trace teachers' perceptions, beliefs, and actions throughout the expulsion process. Their emphasis on "process" is key because, through this analysis, they describe expulsion as not a single, one-time event, but instead as a process shaped over time by adult practices and emotions. In their paper, the study authors describe a process that we have seen play out in vignettes throughout this text in which teachers move through a series of stages which they describe as: Trigger Searching, Intervention Experimentation, Negative Account Making, Ultimatums and Expulsion, and finally, Relief and Regret. The pattern was consistent even when a teacher and program earnestly want to support a child and empathize greatly with a family, as we saw in Jace's story in the prior chapter. This pattern also unfolded very consistently across different types of programs, with more- and less-experienced teachers and in racially homogeneous and diverse settings.

According to Martin and colleagues, the expulsion process begins when a teacher first observes a child's behavior as challenging. Teachers in this study reported being prepared to manage some behavioral issues (many even indicated that it was part of their job to "deal with it") and had tools and strategies to manage the disruptions. However, when the standard strategies did not work, teachers needed to investigate and gain further information about what triggered a specific child's misbehavior. This trigger searching is well exemplified in Jace's story, with both Ms. Elena and the teachers brainstorming how changes in the classroom composition, turnover in the teaching staff, and changes in Jace's home life could all have set him off. Further, they observed a pattern of disruption during and after transitions, and especially on Mondays after spending a weekend away. Likewise, in Noel's story, the teachers at his second program identified several triggers—the noise in the classroom, chaotic transitions, and the time of day all seemed to promote his aggressive behavior.

Teachers interviewed by Martin looked for triggers like those we have reviewed previously—biting may be a symptom of teething in toddlers, frustrated tantrums may be the result of poor fine-motor skills. When teachers could correctly identify and intervene in this triggering (e.g., by proactively assisting a child with fine-motor-demanding tasks like coat zipping), they could help move a child off the path to expulsion. However, when the teachers could not determine the cause of the behavior, they were unable to intervene and felt ineffective, or as Martin and colleagues describe, "these children made their providers feel inadequate and incapable" (2018, pp. 90–91).

This next step in the process often included involving parents and outside experts (e.g., having a child evaluated for services). The more teachers perceived parents to be collaborative partners in their search for an explanation for the behavior, the less likely a child would be expelled. A child's expulsion was accelerated when parents were described as uncooperative, dismissive, or in denial about a child's behavioral challenges. When external evaluations supported and affirmed a teachers' experiences, resulted in concrete and feasible recommendations, and did not detract from their care for other children, teachers reported that the risk of expulsion was mitigated. However, when evaluations conflicted with teachers' perceptions of the child or recommended practices that were onerous or too complex to implement in their classroom, such outside advice could fan the flames of the expulsion process. This is exemplified in Noel's story when his therapist recommended star charts and reinforcements, which clashed with the Montessori pedagogy.

If family and expert involvement did not result in meaningful change in the child's behavior, teachers in this study reported becoming more frustrated and exhausted. As the behavior persisted, they reported much less satisfaction at work, missing more work, and threatening to quit. Martin and colleagues note that at this point in the expulsion cascade, teachers also began to make much stronger negative attributions about children. For example, they used language such as "dangerous" or "unsafe" to describe behavior that has previously just been called "challenging." This negative account-making extended to children's families and home life, and teachers shifted blame for the behavior from the child to the family. Now that the problem fell outside the realm of the child-care setting, however, teachers perceived it as one that was beyond their ability or responsibility to address.

This model of the expulsion process from teachers' perspectives culminates with an ultimatum. The expulsion was not a reaction to a singular event, but instead the result of the clock running out. In most instances, programs gave parents a timeline, for example, 3 weeks, and if the behavior was not improved or some other goal not met, the family was told they needed to find "someplace that better serves his needs" (Martin et al., 2018, p. 94). Although sometimes the parents withdrew their child before that time ran out, there were no instances in which the ultimatum worked—that is, the expulsion was prevented because the behavior changed. Thus, the authors described the ultimatum as functioning just as a means to facilitate the exit of the child, and that it was not intended to serve as an intervention itself. Following the expulsion, teachers being interviewed routinely expressed feeling both intense relief that the process was over and regret that they had not done more. At the same time, many reported feeling as though they had waited too long to expel the child, and there were lingering self-doubts and a depleted sense of self-efficacy.

Throughout the quotes presented in this qualitative study, it is easy to hear the isolation and exhaustion emanating from teachers. As we've seen in prior chapters, early educators are often left ill-equipped and unsupported when it comes to challenging behavior, and the Martin study provides a critical framework for viewing expulsion from the teachers' perspective. Missing from this framework, however, is an account of the role of the program administrator. Although the expulsion process starts inside the classroom with a teacher's observation of a child's behavior, it quickly becomes a program-level challenge, and ultimately, it is the administrator who decides whether a child is retained and accommodated or shown the door.

Decision-Making in the Front Office

Although administrators played significant roles in each of the stories recounted thus far—those of Lance, Elijah, Jace, and Noel—almost no research literature helps us understand the actions of these individuals when it comes to early expulsion. Further, thus far, I have only shared stories of programs that ultimately excluded children, and therefore we cannot determine whether these procedural differences ultimately result in the successful retention of a child.

Each exclusion story has nuances and contextual features, making the identification of a pattern or process particularly difficult. Rather than using case studies as the starting place, I devised a way to more systematically describe the process of exclusion from the program perspective that standardized as much of the context as possible. In 2018, my team and I conducted a series of structured interviews with Illinois-based program administrators.[1]

[1] Details about the methods used in this study can be found in Silver, H. C., Zinsser, K. M., Zulauf-McCurdy, C. A., Lowe-Fotos, A., Orr, L., & Estlund, M. (2021), Transforming early childhood discipline policy through collaborative research and evaluation, *Translational Issues in Psychological Science*, *7*(1), 21–34. https://doi.org/10.1037/tps0000279

Although our sample was small, only 25 administrators, their responses provide a first look at the logistics involved in excluding a child and a possible road map toward interventions. These administrators represented a wide array of programs (Head Starts, community-based preschools, and center-, and home-based child care) and exclusion experiences. Just over half of the programs had excluded a child in the preceding year. As part of the interview, we presented the administrators with a vignette of a child displaying a repeated pattern of challenging behavior. The vignette was adapted from a description used as a prompt in one of Walter Gilliam's experimental studies with teachers, which we will examine more closely in the next chapter. Notably, to avoid triggering implicit biases, we omitted any pronouns or descriptors that would signal a specific gender, race, or ethnicity. A coalition of early childhood experts reviewed the vignette and provided feedback to make sure that it included key behaviors and challenges we have discussed already in this text: aggressive behavior that threatens the safety of others, behavior that is unresponsive to intervention, disruption of normal classroom activities, and teachers' declining sense of efficacy:

> There is a new 4-year-old child in a classroom at your center that displays unpredictable and challenging behaviors. This child has difficulties napping, following instructions, sharing, and taking turns. This child's behavior escalates quickly and disrupts other children's play and learning. On the playground, this child ignores rules about the safe use of the playground equipment and interacts roughly with others, sometimes leaving visible scratches on children's arms. Recently, a teacher reported being kicked repeatedly by this child and feeling unsure about how to handle the behavior and disruption going forward.

During the interviews, we read the vignette and then asked participating administrators how their program would respond if such a child were enrolled in their program. As they answered, we used scripted probes to encourage the administrators to delineate subsequent steps they would take if the behavior persisted. We repeated the probes until the administrator indicated that either the family would voluntarily withdraw the child, or the program would terminate the child's enrollment. We then qualitatively coded their responses for the number, order, and type of steps taken by the administrators. On average, programs would engage in just over seven actions before a child would permanently leave the program, but this number varied widely, with several programs engaging in several iterative cycles of efforts over a longer period, and others taking just five steps within a matter of weeks. We used these reports to construct a conceptual model of administrators' processes, which I envision as happening in parallel with the teacher-level processes described by Martin and colleagues (see Figure 6.1 for combined model).

Most administrators reported that their programs' first response to the vignette would be to either meet with the teachers to devise a strategy or have the teachers observe and record the behavior. About a third of the programs would first try a classroom-based strategy, such as assigning an assistant teacher to shadow the child during challenging transitions. Nearly all programs would have the first meeting with families to discuss the concern. Sometimes this meeting happened before any internal efforts, but most often, it was the second step a program would take. As we saw in Noel's story, some programs used these meetings to gather information and better understand children's behavior at home, or if there is something else that could be causing the child's behavior. Meetings like this often informed a program's next steps. In the stories of Jace and Elijah, we saw Ms. Elena's understanding of their behaviors deepen when the children's home life came into focus.

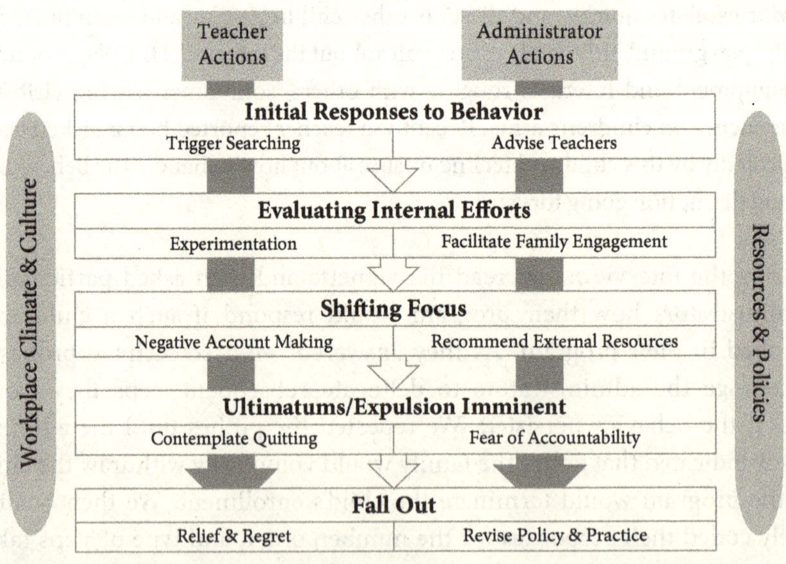

Figure 6.1. Process model for expulsion decision-making within early childhood settings.

Alternatively, though, some interviewed administrators described these family meetings as an opportunity to stress the urgency of the problem. One described the goal as a chance to "give the parents a wake-up call" and set the stage for excluding the child.

When these internal efforts and meetings with the family did not result in a change in the child's behavior, a little less than half of the programs would refer the family to seek outside supports. The most common referrals were to have the child evaluated for early intervention or special education services by the school district. As we saw with Mia, however, this was not always a straightforward request for the family to follow through. About a quarter of programs indicated that they would request the services of a mental health consultant. Consultation is a free service in Illinois available to any early childhood education program (including home-based care) and is designed to aid programs in accommodating and responding to children's behavioral needs. Unfortunately, unless a program had an established relationship with a consultant, many reported that wait times were very long (up to 3 months), making this resource unpractical in emergencies. Notably, except for requests for consultation, when programs sought outside support, it was most often the parent who was left to do the legwork of finding and engaging the resource. Less than half of all of the interviewed administrators indicated that their next response to the vignette would be to implement the advice of the expert. If the behavior persisted, a minority of programs (20%) reported temporarily suspending children, but more often they scheduled follow-up meetings with families. As before, these meetings often served to impress upon the families the seriousness of the program's concerns. Many administrators reported that they would recount what the program has already tried and share documentation with the families, and several indicated that they would give the families warning that if things did not change within a specific time frame, the child would need to leave. Twelve of the 25 administrators reported that they would recommend that the child transition to a new program, and 11 reported that they would terminate the child's enrollment in their program. Two administrators refused to consider the possibility of removing any child from their program regardless of the circumstances.

Regardless of how their responses to the vignette ended, these interviews revealed a pattern. Both those who had and had not expelled a child in the prior year reported that they would typically start with one or two internal efforts, then invite the families in to talk, seek outside supports and services, meet again with families, and then if nothing had improved, the majority would move to exclude. However, within this pattern, there was a great deal of variability in the number of actions taken at each stage in the process, the time and resource costs of these actions, and the responsibility put on the families to follow through on the action. Another critical way in which these administrators' responses differed was in the number of iterations they went through trying out and seeking different solutions. We saw some evidence of these different approaches in Noel's story above. Some programs make quick moves to exclude a child, while others try out multiple strategies over time.

In this interview study, we highlighted the differences in responses to the vignette task by comparing those programs in the bottom and top quartile of counted actions taken. Programs that took only 5 actions in response to the vignette were labeled as "low-effort" responders, and those taking 10 or more were labeled "high-effort" responders. Low-effort responses tended to focus on internal actions and parent actions, as opposed to seeking external assistance and support. These programs made few, if any, references to referrals, evaluations, or the involvement of specialists. Another common theme in this group was the frequent reference to families and parents as "needing to do the work at home." References to the program or staff making internal adjustments to accommodate the child's needs were comparatively rare.

For example, in response to the vignette, one administrator detailed the following response:

ADMIN: If that child was at our program we'd have a meeting with the parent, the teaching team, and me, the director. In that meeting, we would discuss the behavior, what we've seen, find out if the parent is already doing anything at home about it, and make sure the parent is on the same page with us about changing things. We would also devise a plan about how to address it in the classroom. If there's no change in the behavior within a few weeks, we will all meet again and that's when we may recommend that the parents speak with the child's doctor.

INTERVIEWER: And what would the program do if the behavior persisted?

ADMIN: Just really kind of sitting down with the parents [saying it's] not working. We really think that maybe a smaller program or a different type of program would fit your child better.

In this response, you can see that the administrator recounted three steps in their immediate response to the vignette: meet with the family, devise and implement a classroom intervention, meet with the family again and refer to the pediatrician. There was no explicit mention of how the referral to the pediatrician would inform their decision-making process. When the administrator stopped their account, the interviewer only probed once before the administrator indicated that their next step would be the child's exclusion.

By way of contrast, an administrator labeled as "high effort" gave this overview of their hypothetical response to the vignette:

> ADMIN: The first thing we do is we work with the teacher, and we say, "What were the circumstances?" Each one of these incidences had a circumstance, just like napping. You really have to take each one of these incidences by itself because you can't really figure out one thing—one size doesn't fit all. If the teacher always writes that behavior in the report, I would say, "What happened before and after this incident happened?" It could be something to transition. The teacher needs some training in transition. It could be the child doesn't have social-emotional skills. Of course, we ask for early intervention. We have the therapist come in and do observations, and to see what we can do. We already have a mental health specialist that comes in and works with the teacher. . . . And so, that person would come in, and they would say what they thought about it. And then we would get some sort of plan, and we would work with that plan, maybe for the next 10 days and see how it works. And if that didn't work, then we would call the parent in, say, "Anything happening in the home?" 'Cause there's a lot of times there's things that are happening in the home that makes children act out. They just can't say their emotions. So we talk to the parents. And then, at some point, there may be some kind of medical intervention. The doctor would take the behavior reports, and we would send those to the doctor and figure out what he thinks about it. If there's no medical intervention, then we start over again and say, "Well, here's things we're going to do, and here are things we'd like you to do at home, and then we're going to meet back." And then, at some point, it's going to have to be, it's for the safety of the child. That's really the only reason that we would ever expel, is if the child is in danger or other children. The bottom line . . . the parent is involved in the whole process because there can be behavior reports every time. I mean, every day, those behavior reports are sent home. And so, they know things are happening. And the teacher's writing them. And the teacher's talking to me—I'm the

> administrator—about those issues because sometimes they can become pretty disruptive for the class and for other children. And if it keeps just going on and on. First, we have to figure out what we're doing wrong. 'Cause a lot of times it's just teachers that aren't trained correctly [in] how to deal with positively or redirect positively or understand when a child doesn't like people close to them, understand when they're on the spectrum that there are other issues. It could be sensory issues. . . . We're a state board of education Pre-K class. That child, generally, is screened by our special ed department. And if there are so many issues, like the ones that you are talking about that continue, generally, they are moved to a special ed classroom. They go to school instead of onsite here because we don't have any other additional services.

In this response, as in many high-effort responses, the interviewed administrator outlined a more complicated process. This program would go through an internal process that included questioning and investigating the child's behavior and the teachers' reactions, documenting incidents and strategies along the way. They already have a relationship with a consultant and would seek their input before approaching the family. There was a discussion of how their extensive documentation could inform the doctor's evaluation and another family meeting. The description of the family meeting is collaborative, and the administrator reinforced their continual involvement. In the end, this program had easier access to the district's resources and had a clear plan for transitioning the child to special education if they qualified. However, before that point, like many of the high-effort accounts, the administrator described the process as iterative and cited multiple sources of information and feedback. In general, these programs also cited more teacher-level actions and the provision of additional training and support for teachers as needed. Some of these programs also had clearly defined internal steps and interventions that would be implemented before an initial meeting with the family was even scheduled—indicating, possibly, an awareness of the need to more fully understand the challenge and come to the meeting with concrete next steps. High-effort programs in our study also consistently discussed developing an individualized plan with families—as opposed to following a predetermined process and timeline.

Finally, a stark difference between the groups was the laundry list of referenced external resources and supports utilized by these high-effort programs. Administrators who engaged in high-effort responses to the vignette demonstrated an explicit knowledge of the available resources and services in their communities (mental health consultation, speech/language pathology, occupational therapy, specific training for teachers, external evaluators, etc.) and thought creatively about solutions. This interview sample was too small to draw sweeping conclusions, but there was no discernible pattern linking program type to the level of effort detailed by their responses. Publicly and privately funded programs were represented in both groups, and in contrast to my hypotheses, school-based or Head Start programs did not automatically engage in more retention actions.

Programs also differed in their estimate of the duration of how long this process would take. Some programs reported that their program's response to the vignette would conclude within a couple of weeks if families and children were not responsive. Comparatively, some programs—especially those in the high-effort group—reported that when expulsions did occur, they unfolded over months, if not the course of a full school year, which speaks to the intensive nature of the iterative approach. However, even programs expending a great deal of effort and persisting over long periods ultimately admitted that at some point, alternative arrangements would need to be found.

How the child left the program did depend on this effort, however. High-effort administrators, like the second example above, were more likely to end their responses to the vignette by assisting the family with identifying and transitioning their child to another program and sought to make sure that there was no gap in care for the child and family. Low-effort administrators, by comparison, reported that they would terminate enrollment or expel the child outright, akin to Noel's Halloween parade experience. When we cross-referenced their effort level with their reported prior expulsion history, I was at first surprised to see that just like all of the low-effort programs, two-thirds of the programs in the high-effort response group had excluded at least one child in the prior year. As this was a hypothetical scenario and not a recounting of actual events, these findings may be picking up on how prior experience informs programs' development of policies and procedures. For some administrators, the experience of iteratively working with a child and family through challenging behaviors may help inform their toolbox of possible solutions. Through trial and error, these programs have learned about community resources, appropriate interventions, and specific evaluation services. Although both low- and high-effort programs engaged in exclusion, programs that moved more efficiently through the expulsion process did not have time to glean this additional information.

Even from this small study, we gain a glimpse into the myriad of ways programs can approach an exclusion. Programs' differences in their responses to the structured vignette point to possible differences in administrators' management styles and knowledge of resources. Administrators in early childhood education, as in most industries, play a significant role in setting the culture of a workspace. Some administrators may prioritize efficiency, believing that the best course of action for them, their teachers, and the family is to move the child to another care arrangement quickly. These administrators' actions may be motivated by a desire to protect their staff and other children, prevent unnecessary teacher stress, and an honest belief that their program is not well-suited to the child's needs. Unfortunately, as we saw in Lance's story, there is no reason to expect that the next receiving program will be any better prepared to support the child's needs. In fact, it is likely that another program was not the family's first choice for a reason—it may be unaffordable, less accessible, or of lower quality. As we saw in Elijah's story, some children miss out on early education altogether following an expulsion. Nearly a quarter of expelled children in our surveys in Illinois did not find an alternative care arrangement and were kept home instead.

Teachers' experiences and opportunities were at the center of the high-effort example quoted above. In a prior study nearly a decade ago, I conducted focus groups with teachers working in programs that mirror the iterative high-effort programs described above. They consistently reported feeling highly satisfied with their work even when it was difficult. They also reported feeling competent in responding to children's behavior. In contrast, those working where protocols called for efficient inflexible procedures felt powerless and less professional. The slower, more methodical approach to addressing children's challenging behavior may cultivate a climate in which experimentation, trial and error, and collaborative problem-solving are encouraged. These program-level values could benefit a teacher's perceptions of and responses to children's behavior.

In the absence of a supportive workplace climate, however, the benefits of slowing down the process and encouraging iterative experimentation could backfire if teachers experience the iterations as successive failures that are emotionally exhausting. Given that teachers' experiences are situated within the context of a program administrator's approach to exclusion (and management more broadly), overlaying these processes is essential. Figure 6.1 depicts a framework for thinking about the parallel processes described in these two studies. The trigger searching and experimentation stages described in this phenomenological work by Martin, Bosk, and Bailey are akin to some of the procedures described by administrators in our Illinois study. Similarly, the use of ultimatums was evident in several of the administrators' recounts. Finally, both of these models highlight several instances within the process where stronger connections between parents and programs and teachers could interrupt the expulsion cascade. We saw a glimmer of this in Mia and Noel's story, where a communicative assistant teacher helped Mia understand the program's position and reaction to Noel's behavior. Not all programs access or are aware of the available resources in their communities, like mental health consultation, to help guide their work supporting children's behavior. Even if external resources are accessible to teachers, the degree to which they support retention depends on how the program responds. Administrators can play a significant role in guiding teachers to follow through (or not).

In light of what we have already discussed about teachers' workplace experiences and high levels of stress, the emergence of teachers' emotions and sense of efficacy as key components of the expulsion process is not surprising. Administrators' perspectives, beliefs, and feelings appear similarly critical, but we have much less evidence in this area. There were some administrators who expressed concern about the ramifications of not expelling a child quickly enough. They spoke of prioritizing their teachers' well-being, preventing turnover, and fearing that other families would leave the center if the behavior went unchecked.

Another key overlap in these parallel processes was the interaction with parents. Both teachers and administrators pointed to the potential for parents to ameliorate or exacerbate the expulsion process. Both teachers and administrators placed heavy emphasis on being in partnership with parents and wanting parents to collaborate with them. But, as we saw in Noel's story, it is hard to collaborate when you fundamentally don't understand the problem. Further, collaboration was sometimes presented as a one-directional process, with parents being expected to meet the program's definition of engagement. Thinking back to Chapter 4, we can foresee the potential for differences in race, class, and language to further complicate these processes and to mirror broader systems of oppression in our society.

Early childhood professionals cannot avoid interacting with parents. To care for and educate a child is to know and work in partnership with their family and community. We have known for decades that family involvement and engagement with the school are critical ingredients for children's early and continued success. Why then, across all of my interviews with parents, teachers, and administrators, do I routinely hear about parents first being contacted by the program once there is already a problem? If we're truly serious about building partnerships and collaborations, the first call home shouldn't be about a behavior problem. Successful and authentic relationships between home and the program could be conceived as a universal intervention—one that every program can access at nearly no cost—to prevent early childhood expulsion. But what do these relationships look like? And what types of supports do teachers and programs need to forge such connections with families? In our next chapter, we'll explore exactly these questions as we begin to shift our narrative to be solution focused.

7
The Power of Relationships

Roseanne (pseudonym) got into her car, feeling relieved. She opened her laptop and pulled up the state-wide infant and early childhood mental health consultation reporting system and unselected "Retention Threat" from Jiang's status. As she entered notes into the case file about this most recent meeting with center staff and Jiang's parents, she reflected on the hard work that had gotten them to this point. As in most of her cases, Roseanne had been working for several months to cultivate a relationship with this private child-care program. Infant and early childhood mental health consultation was never designed to be a brief intervention, instead relying on relationships, mutual understanding, and trust. As a consultant, Roseanne visits the program regularly, observing and meeting with staff to identify and prioritize their needs and help the program chart a path forward to support children's social-emotional development. Although her efforts are intended to serve as a universal intervention at the program level, it is not uncommon for her to be asked to provide specific advice on supporting an individual child. It was in this role that she was asked to observe a child in the 4-year-old classroom. This boy, Jiang, was constantly moving, struggled to sit on the carpet for morning meetings, and would run back and forth across the room during free-choice or center time. The teachers were exasperated. They felt like they could not take their eyes off him, and his movement was distracting other children as well. Several others in the classroom had started copying his running, and now they had multiple incident reports from children getting hurt bumping into furniture and each other. The teachers had told the parents that the behavior was problematic and sent multiple notes home in his first few weeks in the program. After observing the classroom, Roseanne met with the director when she learned Jiang would likely be asked to leave by the end of the month if something did not change.

Many models of consultation rely on the therapeutic technique of parallel processes. The consultant strives to create a relationship with the administrator that emulates the types of relationships the director can form with teachers and families—one of trust, respect, and patience, which promotes honest communication and accountability. Just as she hoped the administrator would guide a teacher's problem-solving, Roseanne asked the administrator, "What can we do?" and slowly guided her toward identifying some possible steps or actions to prevent Jiang's expulsion. Finally, the administrator suggested trying to meet with the family and working together to understand Jiang's behavior. The director admitted that she was reluctant to work directly with them. English was not the family's primary language, and the teachers reported that the parents always seemed hurried and avoided conversation during pick-up and drop-off. Roseanne's approach to consultation places a heavy emphasis on family engagement. She describes one of her primary jobs as facilitating the programs' ability to build strong relationships between parents and staff. The fact that the parents had not met with the director before concerned her.

She asked if the director could arrange for a family meeting, and the next week, Jiang's mother and father, the classroom teacher, the director, and Roseanne met in the small front office just after morning drop-off. As there were only two adult-sized chairs in the office, Roseanne and the teacher sat on small classroom chairs, and Jiang's father stood against the wall. Roseanne made a mental note about how space may be a factor limiting the administrator's ability to welcome families into the conversation.

Throughout the meeting, Roseanne modeled the same warmth, support, and trustworthiness that she wanted the director to cultivate with her program's families. Her primary goal was to learn the family's story and understand their expectations and hopes for their son. "Stories are so powerful," she explained when we spoke, "stories are the foundation of relationships, and in early childhood, these adult relationships are the real intervention." She elaborated that she sees relationships as "saving space" for the adults to do the hard work of learning and building their shared knowledge of the individual child's needs and strengths. "When there is a good relationship, directors will really take the time to listen to the family to get to know what is going on behind the child's behavior. They are not rushed, and they make sure that substitute teachers are available so that meetings involve teachers too, and no one is distracted."

Roseanne worked to create that space and time in this meeting, to help the director and teacher learn Jiang's family story. Jiang was born in China, in the city of Guangzhou, one of the most crowded and populated cities in the world. His family immigrated to the United States when he was almost 2. He was an only child, and his parents raised him alone; all four of Jiang's grandparents died before he was born. Jiang learned how to walk very late, just around the time they were moving to America. The parents did not initially seem distressed by this delay and admitted that his limited mobility was somewhat convenient because they lived in a single room in Guangzhou, and a busy mobile toddler would have been hard to contain. Here in the United States, Jiang's parents described expending a great deal of energy trying to contain Jiang. They still lived in a small apartment and wanted him to be still and calm while at home. Slowly a picture emerged for Roseanne, and she could see in the faces of the teachers and administrators an expanded understanding of Jiang's behavior. With its bright sunny hallways and open-concept classrooms, the child-care center was comparatively immense, and to Jiang likely looked custom-built for running.

By learning his story and understanding more about his home life, the program staff began to shift from viewing Jiang as a problem to seeing his energy and clumsiness as natural expressions of his developmental experiences. When the program had located the problem in Jiang, only his removal would "solve" it. With the telling of his story, however, the program staff began to locate the problem in the environment, that it was not well suited to support Jiang's behavioral regulation. These teachers were well-versed in adapting classroom environments, and they were now able to think creatively about solutions to which they already had access. Roseanne reported that the energy in the small office quickly shifted as the teachers and director started brainstorming new strategies to try: Maybe they could rearrange the daily schedule so that outside time came earlier in the day or more frequently? Could furniture in the classroom be rearranged so that there was not a long clear path for running? Were there more gross-motor free-choice activities that could be added to the lesson plan? Could they build a sensory walk or obstacle course with tape in the hallway and allow Jiang to expend energy throughout the day?

Roseanne also knew that the family and program would benefit from resources and support around motor delays and help understand developmentally appropriate expectations for children's energy and need for movement. However, all of this would take time—months, actually—months that, before this family meeting, Jiang would not have had as a student at this center. Roseanne knew that lasting change had occurred when she came back to do a follow-up visit just before the winter holiday break. Jiang's classroom teacher excitedly showed her a map she had proactively drawn of all of the neighborhood playgrounds his parents could take him to during the vacation, "so he can get his wiggles out!"

* * *

My summary of this story is ultimately too simplistic. Roseanne's work started well before she met Jiang's family, and this single family meeting was not a panacea to all of the program's challenges. But it was a start, and it exemplified how empathizing with and understanding children and families can interrupt expulsion processes. Throughout this text, I have continually highlighted the centrality of emotion in the expulsion pipeline. Children's emotions underscore the behaviors that are deemed challenging. Teachers' emotional exhaustion leaves them vulnerable to cognitive shortcuts. Fear of accountability challenges teacher and administrator decision-making. It is only fitting, then, that empathy, or one's ability to understand and share another's feelings, may prove to be a key component in the path toward retention.

Roseanne's intentional efforts to ensure that the program heard and understood Jiang's story was an important step toward building or reigniting the staffs' empathic response. This is not to say that the teachers were not caring and compassionate people who ultimately wanted what was best for Jiang. In fact, you would be hard-pressed to find someone working in helping or person-centered professions, like nursing or teaching, who was not motivated by their strong empathic responses to others' needs. However, as has been well documented across disciplines, these professionals are also vulnerable to compassion fatigue (Stebnicki, 2008). There is even some evidence that teachers burn out more quickly than those in other helping professions due to their prolonged interactions with students (compared with the shorter-term or intermittent interactions of nurses, counselors, etc.; De Heus & Diekstra, 1999).

The role of empathy in exclusionary discipline was demonstrated in an online intervention designed by Jason Okonofua, David Panuesku, and Gregory Walton at Stanford University. To reduce the use of suspension by middle-school teachers, Okonofua and colleagues (2016) developed a brief two-part training that reinforced a message of the value of supportive relationships and respect for students' experiences and feelings. Teachers listened to recorded stories from students about how positive relationships with teachers impacted them, and teachers wrote short essays ostensibly to share with more junior teachers about how they would incorporate these ideas into their regular teaching practice. Despite the brevity and simplicity of the intervention, these activities had positive effects. Students whose teachers received the empathic-mindset intervention were half as likely to be suspended over the school year than students whose teachers were in the control group. These effects persisted even after the researchers controlled for student race, gender, and any prior disciplinary exclusions. Priming teachers' empathic attending to students' emotional experiences in the classroom was especially potent for students who traditionally are more likely to be excluded. Boys, Black or Latino children, and those who had been suspended in the past were half as likely to be suspended in the treatment versus control classrooms.

Thinking through the potential adaptation of such an intervention for early childhood spaces, we immediately run into a logistical challenge. Young children cannot articulate their stories and the influence of caring relationships as convincingly as middle schoolers. Instead, infants, toddlers, and preschoolers are dependent on the adults in their lives to communicate on their behalf. While parents loom large in all education settings, their role is especially critical and developmentally necessary in early childhood. That is, teaching is facilitated by both the teacher-child relationship and the parent-teacher relationship.

In the ecological model that framed our investigation initially, the connection between home and school sits in Bronfebrenner's "mesosystem": the place between the most proximal influences in a child's development (parents, siblings, and home) and the slightly more distal systems (like schools, churches, and cultural institutions) with which they interact as they grow and develop. In the mesosystem, the individuals who separately care for and support a child's development (e.g., their parents, teachers, and coaches) interact with each other on behalf of the child. The degree to which these spheres of influence in a child's life interact and the tenor of these interactions are associated with children's social, behavioral, and academic success.

When parents and teachers form collaborative, positive relationships, children thrive. When these interactions are adversarial or are focused on blaming, children experience more negative feedback and less support overall at school. These effects are especially potent in early childhood (Lang et al., 2017), in part because young children cannot self-advocate and are dependent on adults to know what and when to communicate on their behalf. When a parent can share information about a child's home life (e.g., a child's sleep patterns, the arrival of a new sibling, a parent's absence) or individual characteristics like their fears and worries, interests, and successful soothing techniques, teachers may be able to better understand, predict, and sympathize with a child's behavior. Similarly, when teachers share classroom activities, tendencies, and challenges, and when parents are involved in their child's early education, both sides can work together to benefit the child's social-emotional development.

As we will see in this chapter's unfolding pages, exclusionary discipline in early childhood may be a family affair. Roseanne's story emphasized the importance of teachers understanding children's stories as the basis for cultivating empathy and motivation to persist in working with children who display challenging behaviors. Her professional experience echoed reports of teachers' and administrators' experiences of the expulsion process described in the previous chapter. Parents are integral to the expulsion process, whether they know it or not. Lance's and Noel's parents knew that their reputations in the eyes of the teacher mattered. Both parents spoke of trying to build good graces proactively. Stephen, Lance's father, even ordered lunches for the teaching staff at one child-care center to forestall his son's eventual exclusion. But we should not be relying on a few pizzas to prevent expulsion. We also cannot rely only on stories. As we begin to shift our collective gaze toward intervention and prevention efforts in the concluding chapters of this text, we must look beyond the school building and consider the role of the broader community context in the expulsion cascade. To start, we will more carefully examine the context of the relationship between home and school, the direct and indirect roles these relationships play in expulsion decision-making, and how we can leverage these relationships as a universal strategy.

Roseanne knew that engaging Jiang's family in conversation with his teachers was the most crucial first step toward preventing his expulsion. The importance of building rapport with families and encouraging their involvement in early education is common knowledge among practitioners and has been reinforced by nearly 50 years of research. When programs and teachers open doors for parents' active involvement in their child's early education, children thrive. When there are open lines of communication and teachers and parents can collaborate to develop shared expectations for children's learning and behavior (deemed "goodness-of-fit" by Churchill, 2003), children score higher on measures of social competence over time, and there is a lasting positive impact on their academic achievement (Ryan et al., 1995). Parent-teacher relationships built around comfort, communication, and consistency are associated with better social, behavior and academic child outcomes (see Smith et al., 2020, for a full review).

Encouraging and facilitating parental involvement is even codified in federal policy and definitions of program quality. For example, Parts B and C of the Individuals with Disabilities Education Improvement Act of 2004 (IDEA) requires that schools must facilitate family engagement for children with disabilities by providing a range of services for parents, including training, counseling, and transportation (Brotherson et al., 2008). Policies governing Head Start likewise stipulate that programs must establish and maintain family partnerships and provide services such as training and translation to support parents' participation. Private programs must also demonstrate effective home-school relationships as part of meeting the quality standards for accreditation by the National Association for the Education of Young Children (NAEYC). At the local level, many states' teaching performance standards likewise emphasize skills around building and maintaining these relationships. For example, in Illinois, the Gateways credentialing system for early educators includes seven competencies around collaborating with families, including implementing culturally and linguistically appropriate procedures to learn about and act on families' goals for their children (https://www.ilgateways.com/).

Unfortunately, even though practitioners "know" the value of these relationships with families, there is little explicit guidance about how to facilitate this relationship. Many teachers report that it is challenging to involve families at a level that would benefit children (Ratcliff & Hunt, 2009). Further, even when teachers believe they have established meaningful relationships with the parents they serve, parents report the opposite (Torres, 2019). In fact, many parents report that they are rarely consulted on important issues about their child's schooling (Lawson, 2003). Research has further revealed that parents and teachers have different understandings of what constitutes involvement in their child's education. Teachers tend to expect parents to engage in school-centric activities, such as volunteering in the classroom or serving on committees. Conversely, parents speak of home-centric activities like talking with their children about what they are learning in school, reinforcing literacy, and encouraging children to listen to and respect their teachers (Coba-Rodriguez et al., 2020). This disconnect tends to also fall along racial and ethnic lines, with non-Hispanic White families engaging in more of the school-centric activities valued by teachers. Without open communication opportunities, teachers and parents have no way to develop a relationship that would enable them to have vulnerable conversations about goals for or concerns about a child's development. As we have seen in many of the stories recounted thus far, too often, the first time a teacher opens a direct line of communication with a family it is to report that their child's behavior is unacceptable. Although it may be common knowledge that positive parent-teacher relationships are essential, we cannot guarantee that they will naturally happen. In studying this vital relationship between home and school, it is increasingly evident that we have failed to invest in creating conditions that can support parents and teachers working together. In the ensuing vacuum, the lack of a relationship (at best) or an adversarial one instead appears to serve as a direct contributor to children's exclusion.

As we saw in the previous chapter, teachers' interactions with and decisions about children who may be expelled are tied closely to their perceptions of parents. Both administrators and teachers interviewed about the expulsion process highlighted how parents' actions could shift the expulsion course. But in reality, parents hold very little power in the home-school relationship, especially if they face arbitrary ultimatums. Therefore, we must understand how teachers' perceptions of parents form and how to support positive partnerships that in turn contribute to children's early development.

Teachers' perceptions of parents directly impact their interactions with children. When parents are viewed positively, preschool teachers report less conflict with the child (Serpell & Mashburn, 2012) and perceive the child as displaying fewer problem behaviors (Gregory et al., 2010). If a teacher likes the child's parent, it may increase the amount of time that teacher spends with the child in the classroom, improve the quality of interactions between the teacher and the child, and reduce the likelihood that the teacher labels the child as having behavioral problems (Serpell & Mashburn, 2012). This positive reinforcement and feedback loop likely explain why children score higher on later assessments of academic and social success when teachers and parents get along (Herman & Reinke, 2017).

In contrast, if a teacher has a negative perception of a child's parents, they are at greater risk of being expelled. That was one of the key findings of a study directed by Courtney Zulauf-McCurdy at the University of Illnois at Chicago. Nearly 300 preschool teachers completed surveys about children in their classes who had and had not previously been expelled from other programs, including perceptions of their relationships with the child's parents and the degree to which the child was at risk of being expelled. This study's results were the first to demonstrate that children's expulsion risk was significantly and inversely correlated with teachers' relationships with parents. Teachers reported having more negative relationships with parents of children who were at greater risk of being expelled in the future. They disagreed with statements about support and agreement (e.g., "This parent makes me feel like I am the best possible teacher for his/her child" and "This parent and I have the same goals for his/her child"), and agreed more strongly with items about undermining interactions (e.g., "This parent does not trust my abilities as a teacher").

Unfortunately, teachers' perceptions of parents are subject to the same implicit biases as our broader society, including racism and classism. Teachers are more likely to perceive low-income, less well-educated, and racially minoritized parents as less involved and less cooperative than their middle-class White peers (Hauser-Cram et al., 2003; Nzinga-Johnson et al., 2009). Zulauf-McCurdy traced this bias against parents to a child's expulsion risk. In a follow-up analysis, she found that the parent-teacher relationship was a much stronger predictor of expulsion risk for Black children than non-Black children who had not been expelled. That is, teachers' negative perceptions of parents place Black children at a significantly higher risk of a first-time expulsion in the future than their non-Black peers.

Trying to understand how these negative perceptions form, Kathryn Howard and Sarah Lipinoga from the University of Pennsylvania (2010) studied Mexican-origin families' experiences during kindergarten parent-teacher conferences. Teachers perceived that parents' lack of questions was an indication that they were disengaged in their child's education. However, these same parents reported perceiving the teachers' rushed demeanor and use of jargon as dismissive and were hesitant to prolong the conference by asking questions about their child's progress. The authors suggest that the conferences are not only a missed opportunity for rapport building, but the lack of communication and subsequent misinterpretation by teachers feeds into a stereotype that Latino parents are not interested in being involved in their child's schooling. Over time, teachers' accumulated experiences and misperceptions of parents' interest lead teachers to generalize these negative impressions across families. As a result, teachers may invest less effort in engaging families of backgrounds different from their own.

Just as perceptions of specific children's parents impact their risk of expulsion, these generalized stereotypes seem to bleed over to affect other children's futures as well. Specifically, in an analysis of data from my Chicago area teacher study (Zulauf & Zinsser, 2019), we found that early childhood teachers who had requested an expulsion in the prior year endorsed more negative perceptions of parents in general. They agreed more strongly with statements such as "It is difficult to get parents to be consistent with me in dealing with children" and "It is difficult to get parents to work with me on behavior problems" than teachers who had not requested an expulsion. In follow-up interviews, teachers who had and had not requested expulsions spoke differently about how and when they engage families. Teachers who had previously expelled a child attributed children's challenging behavior to parental characteristics more frequently and in greater detail than teachers who had not requested an expulsion. In discussing children's behavior, two-thirds of teachers who had expelled a child made unsolicited negative comments about parents, including references to poor mental health, history with the criminal justice system, and marital status. These negative accounts are akin to those reported by Martin and colleagues (2018) in their interview of preschool teachers in Michigan (see Chapter 6). Importantly, in this study, teachers are rating their perceptions of parents in general, not only those of children expelled. That is, these teachers with expulsion experience carried more negative global perceptions of parents.

This perceptual bias likely explains the related difference we found in their styles of communication with families. The majority of teachers who had recently expelled a child in this study also expressed a limited communication style with families. As one teacher said, "The last thing I think about when having to deal with a child's behavior . . . is talking to the parents." Another indicated that she "only communicates [with parents] when it is a certain behavior such as hitting." In contrast, those who had not expelled a child reported "creating as many excuses as we can to get close to parents" and being "really proactive" in communicating with parents. Others offered advice saying that they had to "find a balance with letting [the parent] know all of the wonderful things [the child] is doing, while at the same time being honest." Another reminded herself to not "get impatient or angry because they are not listening to you . . . just keep communicating with the family."

When parents are viewed negatively by teachers, they may receive differential treatment from both the teacher and center, such as less frequent and meaningful communication and less cooperation and partnership for helping a child persist in a classroom (Lott, 2001). As a result, children and parents who may need the most positive attention and support to engage them in education are the ones who are likely to be viewed least favorably by teachers (Downer & Myers, 2010).

Walter Gilliam and Chen Reyes designed an experiment to better test whether and how knowing more about a child's parents influenced teachers' discipline decisions. In this study, teachers read a vignette describing a child displaying unpredictable and challenging behaviors (e.g., pushing children, hitting staff when frustrated) and difficulty regulating his/her attention and behavior (e.g., waiting for turns, speaking out of turn). The vignettes were identical except that Gilliam manipulated the child's gender and race using stereotypical Black and White girl and boy names (Latoya, Emily, DeShawn, Jake) and related pronouns. In addition, half of the participating teachers in the study also received additional information about the child's family intended to approximate the types of information a teacher would typically garner through interacting with a child's family over a year:

> [CHILD NAME] lives with his/her mother, his/her 8- and 6-year-old sisters, and his/her 10-month-old baby brother. His/her home life is turbulent, between having a father who has never been a constant figure in his/her life, and a mother who struggles with depression but doesn't have the resources available to seek help. During the rare times when his/her parents are together, loud and sometimes violent disputes occur between them. In order to make ends meet, [CHILD's] mother has taken on three different jobs, and is in a constant state of exhaustion. [CHILD] and his/her siblings are left in the care of available relatives and neighbors while their mother is at work.

After reading the vignettes, teachers completed a short survey where they rated the severity of the child's behavior, the degree to which they believed that nothing could be done to improve the child's behavior (hopelessness), and the likelihood they would recommend the child be suspended/expelled. The experimental manipulation ensures that the differences in ratings are due to teachers' differing perceptions. Overall, participants who received more information about the family's background indicated feeling more hopeless about the prospects of the child's behavior improving. This effect of teacher hopelessness is akin to the processes described by teachers being interviewed by Martin and colleagues. Hopelessness has also been quantified empirically as a predictor of expulsion risk (Gilliam & Reyes, 2018). Especially for teachers in under-resourced or overcrowded classrooms, the realization that a child's behavior stems from a complex and seemingly insurmountable list of other needs appears to be enough to lead teachers to throw up their hands.

An additional finding of this experimental study was that teachers' perceptions of the severity of children's behavior systematically varied by whether the teacher had additional information about the family, and importantly, by teacher and child race. When Black teachers were provided with additional family background information for Black children, they rated children's behavior as significantly less severe than when they did not have additional family information. However, when that same background information was provided about Black children to White teachers, severity ratings increased compared to teachers' ratings when no background information was provided. Gilliam and colleagues hypothesize that while there is a tendency for teachers to show greater empathy for others' misfortune, empathy is primarily reserved for people of their own race. Therefore, it is possible that White teachers are overwhelmed by the additional family information for Black children, while Black teachers are better able to empathize with the familial stresses.

Beyond this experimental manipulation, parent and teacher ethnic match might increase the parent's comfort in interacting with the classroom teacher, resulting in more parent engagement. When teachers and parents share ethnic identities, parents are more likely to report higher levels of engagement compared to mismatched dyads (Mundt et al., 2015). Unfortunately, teachers are not consistently trained to develop relationships with parents of different ethnic, cultural, and linguistic backgrounds (Smith & Sheridan, 2019). Instead, when teachers and families lack shared identities, teachers may behave more like the teachers in my Chicago study—avoiding communication with families and missing out on opportunities to build rapport. As we saw in Chapter 5, working conditions place teachers at risk of making quick judgments. Both my study and Gilliam's work show that in the absence of open communication and limited information, these judgments are vulnerable to stereotypes.

Despite a convergence around the important role that teachers' perceptions of and relationships with parents play in preventing or disrupting expulsion, significant barriers remain in promoting these types of relationships in early childhood settings. One barrier is that a one-size-fits-all approach will not work. Just as instruction needs to be individualized to support children's learning, so too, it appears, will teachers need to adapt their styles of interacting with families for each individual parent.

In her 2019 study, Luz Torres found that parents in the same Head Start classroom had widely different perspectives of their relationships with their child's teacher and reported statistically unrelated levels of comfort. That is, even in the same classroom with the same resources and theoretically the same opportunities for interaction, parents have different experiences working with their child's teacher.

Another barrier is that teachers' use of family-centric practices appears unrelated to their training and experience. In that same study with 227 teachers and 747 parents in Head Start classrooms, Torres found that teachers' engagement in family-centered practices (such as collaboration, communication, and responsiveness) was not explained by their level of education, years of experience, or training to work with children and families who spoke a language other than English at home. In contrast to the conclusions drawn by Gilliam and colleagues above about the importance of shared identities, in this sample, teachers' engagement in these practices was not explained by their racial/ethnic background or if their background matched their students' backgrounds. This divergence could be explained by the fact that Torres included parents' report of specific teacher practices as opposed to broad statements about engagement.

Instead, regarding factors that promote better perceptions of parents and stronger parent-teacher relationships to reduce expulsions, the evidence we do have points toward the role of the administration. For example, in our Chicago area study, the same teachers who had previously expelled a child and held negative perceptions of parents in general also reported feeling unsupported by their programs (Zulauf & Zinsser, 2019). Specifically, they disagreed more strongly with statements like "My program supports staff in their efforts to engage parents" and "My program promotes cooperation between teachers and parents" compared to teachers who had not expelled any children. In the qualitative follow-up interviews, those with no expulsion history spoke of their directors as positive supports for dealing with challenging behavior in the classroom and helping them communicate with parents. The directors' ability to help the teachers and communicate with parents seemed to unburden teachers in this group. Others in this group indicated that the administrator had established a culture that valued parent involvement. As one said, "There's nothing written, it's just our philosophy. We just want to help each and every child [who is] failing. So, I mean it's an unwritten policy that we work with the parents."

In contrast, teachers who had expelled a child described their directors as unhelpful or likely to put the work back on them. This may reflect a larger problem at the center level, that teachers are overburdened and do not have the capacity to work with parents. The extent that administrators create a climate and culture of open communication and family engagement appear associated with teachers' perception of parents and use of exclusionary discipline.

We get a fuller picture of how administrative actions can promote or hinder parent-teacher relationships in a follow-up investigation a few years later. Zulauf-McCurdy led a qualitative study of teachers and parents to identify components of relationships that each attributed to preventing a child's expulsion. She conducted in-depth interviews with a sample of parents whose children had previously been expelled and teachers who had taught children with prior expulsion histories. To our knowledge, this is the only study that specifically assessed parents' experiences of the parent-teacher relationship leading up to a preschool expulsion. Both parents and teachers also answered questions about how their prior experiences informed their future interactions and what challenges still exist.

Among the findings were consistent themes from both teachers and parents around barriers to communication and relationship formation. One teacher explained that her director was "definitely encouraging us to have regular conversations [with families] . . . but our staffing models make it tricky." Both parents' and teachers' work schedules precluded them from having timely conversations. To work a 9–5 job, parents often have to drop their children off at childcare before 8 a.m. and pick them up after commuting home. Lead teachers typically work the same 8-hour day as parents and are often not the ones in the classroom when children are dropped off or collected. Instead, an assistant or part-time teacher covers the early morning and evening shifts. In addition to a lack of face-time, teachers cannot easily step out of the classroom to make a phone call to a parent if an issue arises. In many instances, communication either happens through less personal media (like text or email after hours) or as messages passed on by assistant teachers who did not witness the incident directly. Even when teachers' and parents' schedules did overlap, attempts to talk during pick-up or drop-off times were universally described as unsuccessful. Parents were rushed to get to work or home and teachers were distracted by other children's needs. Finally, if they could find a quiet moment, both parents and teachers were hesitant to have conversations in front of the child.

These findings point to unintended consequences of business decisions and ratio requirements in early childhood programs. As we discussed in Chapter 5, early childhood work is highly structured, and teachers have little autonomy to choose how to invest their time, contributing to workplace stress. We can see how this lack of flexibility also detracts from relationship formation with families.

Despite the complexities of communication, nearly all participants in Zulauf-McCurdy's interviews echoed the results shared above about establishing early lines of communication before behavior challenges emerge. One solution posited by several parents and teachers in this study was for administrators and programs to arrange for time for teachers to meet with parents informally at the time of admission. Importantly, these meetings were not about giving the parents information about the program or curriculum; they were unstructured chances to get to know one another. As one described, "We invited him and his parents to come in to meet myself and my co-teacher at a time when there were no other students or adults in the room. . . . Then that also gave us a chance to chat with the parents a little bit more and see how they interacted with him and chat about what they know works for him and things like that."

From the parents' perspective, the value of these meetings was in how they set a tone for all future interactions. One parent explained how fulfilling it was to have a teacher earnestly want to know more about their daughter. "The teacher asked open-ended questions like . . . 'What are your favorite things about her? What's her favorite thing to do? What's her least favorite thing to do?' She really got a full picture."

In many ways, these informal getting-to-know-you visits hearken back to the nursery school tradition of home visits. My own mother used to do home visits when she taught kindergarten at Grace Church School in Brooklyn, New York, and they were always her favorite part of the school year. Beyond meeting children before the start of the year, she thought that there was real value in learning about what home was like for them and how they acted in a familiar and comfortable place. While home visits may not be feasible (or may even undercut some relationships if families feel like they are being spied on or evaluated), similar proactive strategies, such as park meet-ups, classroom visits, or video conferences, can help teachers and parents start on the right foot.

When parent-teacher communication begins after a teacher is concerned about the behavior, the conversation is likely to be negative in nature, thus deterring from mutual understanding and partnership. In contrast, parent-teacher communication that begins early and is positive in nature can foster the development of a robust parent-teacher relationship (Lang et al., 2017). As Walter Gilliam quipped during a conversation at the Yale Child Study Center in 2019, you never see a child expelled when the parent and teacher like each other. Early communication may be something easy to promote that has a lasting impact. Even in the absence of a scheduled family visit, teachers who intentionally communicate something positive with every family within the first days of school can start relationships on a positive note and indicate that they are willing to include parents in the learning process. Signaling a desire to build a relationship may go a long way toward parents reciprocating and breaking down negative feedback loops in early childhood.

It is important to remember, however, that parent-teacher relationships are transactional; both parties have a role to play in setting the tone and building rapport. Most importantly, parents should be open-minded and willing to engage with teachers to help them best support the child. In the absence of a relationship, when teachers do reach out, they are often confronted with defensive parents. Teachers in Zulauf-McCurdy's study, as well as those described by Martin (2018; see Chapter 6) and our Chicago area teachers, all recounted how hard it is to talk with a parent who is in denial about their child's behavior. These teachers spoke of anticipating and dreading the conflict that would arise when they brought a concern to the families, and some even put off the interaction for as long as possible. What may be unclear to parents is that children's biting, hitting, and defiant behaviors are developmentally typical and do not reflect poorly on them as parents. It is hard not to feel under the microscope when your child misbehaves. You know this keenly if your child has ever had a tantrum in public. But if teachers can approach these conversations from a non-judgmental stance and parents can remain open-minded, communication can blossom. Parents' reactions to a teachers' first attempt to talk about a child's behavior go a long way in setting the tone and likelihood of future communication. Across Zulauf-McCurdy's interviews, parents agreed that they would rather have an open conversation early on than have the teachers avoid bringing it up until it's too late.

From the program side, administrators can do a great deal to grease the cogs of these parent-teacher interactions by normalizing the need for teachers to reach out for insight and help with a child's behavior. Through their handbooks and admission processes, some programs signal clearly that parents are the greatest experts on their children and that teachers are eager to learn about what works for them at home. Acknowledging that all children will struggle emotionally or behaviorally at some point and proactively seeking parents' input is another approach. Some programs I've worked with also ask all new parents to sign waivers that allow teachers to seek expert advice or have a specialist observe their interactions with a child (e.g., mental health consultants, speech/language pathologists, and occupational therapists). These observations can give teachers important tools and resources, but many parents' fears of being signaled out may inhibit the school gaining consent later on. When everyone is asked to sign the waiver, these programs are trying to reduce the stigma of having a "challenging" child.

The final findings from Zulauf-McCurdy's study reiterate these calls for open, honest communication. From the parents' perspective, they wanted early communication about any challenges in the classroom; "please do not sweep them under the rug," one pleaded. Many parents believed that being left in the dark about the severity of their child's needs contributed to their ultimate expulsion. For example, one shared, "Part of the issue that we've had [with the previous teacher] is that we were not kept abreast of the difficulties that were arising until it was pretty much well on its way. For several weeks there was no direct communication."

At the same time, teachers were sensitive to not being too negative, and many emphasized being sure to balance the types of information communicated with parents. Even though it was challenging, one teacher underscored the importance of "always giving some positive feedback, even on the hardest of days." When teachers and parents can interact and communicate openly, they build impressions of each other as partners. This rapport may be the key that holds the relationship together if and when more challenging conversations need to occur later.

Learning is a social process tied to the relationships and interactions among individuals. From Vygotsky's early writings through today's expansive research into student-teacher relationship quality, we have seen that positive, caring, and supportive interactions promote achievement and motivation and perseverance in the face of challenges. As we saw in the Stanford empathy intervention study, even the reminder of the importance of relationships can also promote teachers' learning to adapt their discipline styles. However, in early childhood, we must also expand our thinking about the influence of these social processes to reach outside of the classroom walls.

As the studies and stories shared in this chapter have highlighted, the social interactions between home and school (or the lack thereof) can, directly and indirectly, support child and teacher behavior and children's retention. We have also seen how the components of the ecological settings surrounding these dyadic social processes influence their tenor and openness. Administrative practices and management of resources, time, and staff may promote or inhibit relationship formation. Administrators can also create a culture that acknowledges the developmentally appropriate expectations for children's behavior and reduces the stigma and defensiveness around parent-teacher collaboration to address challenges. Likewise, societal factors like perceptual biases and teachers' and parents' past experiences influence their willingness to take advantage of opportunities to relate.

If these social processes—among and between teachers, children, families, and program administration—are key to preventing expulsion, we need to explore ways to support and promote these interactions more intentionally. In the next chapter, we will look at promising approaches to facilitate these social processes and what it will take to implement such interventions at scale.

8
Promising Pathways Forward

I sat with Katie Conklin, the executive director of Tuesday's Child, on low love seats at the behavioral intervention program's entrance. Despite the green tulle draped from the ceiling and rain forest motif, it was hard to overlook the building's history as a high school. Conklin is a young executive who started as an intern and worked her way up through the organization, which relies on a dedicated staff of only 15 to serve nearly two thousand families each year. "I painted the walls in that classroom myself!" she said, capturing the many-hands mentality of the program.

Tuesday's Child offers three primary services: a short intensive behavioral intervention, an onsite therapeutic preschool program, and community-based positive parenting workshops. Their founding program, the behavioral intervention program, started nearly 40 years ago as a dissertation project of Victoria Lavigne and Katherine Augustyn, graduate students studying mental health care and early childhood education (ECE). Their goal was to assist families of young children who had conflict-ridden relationships. The original model is still in use today and combines intensive small group positive parenting training and classroom-based behavioral intervention for preschool-age children.

Conklin described how their program serves as the final option for many Chicago area families who have experienced exclusion. "About 60% of our families have been asked to leave at least one preschool program by the time they come to us. Often it is more like two or three programs. . . . Sometimes parents are told that if they want to keep their child at the child care program, they personally have to hire a dedicated aide." Children who arrive at Tuesday's Child are similar to the stories we have seen throughout this book, "they are biting, aggressive, and struggle to regulate their emotions. Often, they are diagnosed with oppositional defiance disorder, autism spectrum disorder, or ADHD for insurance purposes."

In the Tuesday's Child intervention model, parents and children come to the program once a week for 12 weeks. Parents learn to replace ineffective parenting strategies with positive behavior management techniques to change their children's inappropriate behaviors throughout these two-and-a-half-hour-long sessions. Peer mentors and group counseling from a clinical psychologist help parents develop confidence and knowledge on topics ranging from developing and sustaining behavioral modification plans to developmental and intellectual disabilities. Sessions on nutrition, bedtime routines, and child abuse prevention also help parents anticipate and monitor sources of stress in the home. A powerful component of the program is the training parents receive in advocacy; parents learn a lot about their child's rights under the Americans with Disabilities Act, like how to interpret an Individualized Education Plan (IEP), and how to access the services they need. This training will enable them to advocate on behalf of their child for years to come.

The program is grounded in the functional family systems theory, positing that individuals are inseparable from their relationships with others. "There are not really any other programs like us around here," Conklin said, explaining that most other programs focus on just the parent or just the child. Some challenges are logistical; in order to work with whole family units, the families must juggle schedules and make it possible to attend these lengthy sessions during work hours. Traditional parenting training programs can be run in the evenings; child-only interventions can be delivered at school or not require parent presence. Tuesday's Child has made modifications over the years to better facilitate whole family involvement, including adding a condensed weekends-only version of the intervention.

While the parents are working together with the counselor, children spend time in the classroom. Very small ratios (four or fewer children per adult) and teachers with advanced training are at the core of the program's success. Teachers use behavioral techniques such as redirecting, praising, and rewards to promote children's time on task, social skills, and compliance. "We use Skittles and M&Ms. Some folks may raise an eyebrow at that, but we are looking to raise [children's] confidence and give them positive feedback." There is a large emphasis on structure and choice to provide opportunities and support for children's innate drive for exploration. A predictable structure helps reduce anxiety and facilitates children's focused attention on learning activities designed to promote social proficiency and school readiness.

Each year, the behavioral intervention program serves 250 families. A sliding scale fee based on family income and separate groups for Spanish-speaking families make the program more accessible. "Some families pay only $5 a week to attend. We used to make it free, but we realized that if they didn't have anything invested, attendance would fall off. . . . Otherwise, we are funded by donations, tuition, and fund-raising drives." Regardless, the cost and the time demands *can be barriers to some families, especially those dependent on full-time care. "Some families are so desperate for help that they'll take FMLA (unpaid family medical leave) to have time off work while going through the program. But it's worth it to them." Evaluations of the program have shown that it does indeed have lasting impacts on children and families. Among those who complete the Behavior Intervention program, Conklin explained, "half of the children leaving the intervention transition back into a traditional preschool and thrive there. The other half, we refer out and help them transition into the school district special education program." Both parents and Tuesday's Child teachers rate children's behavior as significantly better after the 12-week intervention. Children who rarely, if ever, took turns or resolved conflicts with words instead of physical aggression were rated as often or always doing so by their parents and teachers after the program. Similarly, children improved their ability to follow directions, comply with requests to clean up, and smoothly transition from one activity to another.*

Tuesday's Child's website is full of happy family portraits of success stories. For example, the Tripp family shared that their son, Thomas, was "out of control." He had been kicked out of preschool and was not welcome at swim class anymore. He was in all the therapies the doctor recommended. His father recounts how Tuesday's Child's approach differed: "The focus was on learning parenting skills for children who have behavior problems. We weren't focusing on fine motor skills or speech. We were focusing on Thomas as a person and us as a family. I learned to observe Thomas's behavior and see it as a form of communication. . . . I learned that my job was to stay calm and be patient. That in being calm and patient, I could use techniques I was learning at Tuesday's Child and quickly manage a meltdown. I gained confidence in my ability to parent Thomas and the ability to handle every situation that came my way. Eventually, Thomas learned to ask for help when he was frustrated and used his angry words when he got mad. He learned to be a good friend and how to learn in a classroom. We learned how to be a happy family again."

* * *

Therapeutic interventions like Tuesday's Child play a critical role in supporting families during and after the expulsion, and it is not surprising how much relief the families exude in testimonials. At the same time, this approach can only support a small number of families and requires a significant time commitment. Additionally, it places the burden for change on the child and the parents. In his book, *The Troubled and Troubling Child*,

child psychologist Nicholas Hobbs wrote, "The way one defines a problem will determine in large measure the strategies used to solve it" (1982, p. 182). In stand-alone therapeutic preschool programs and interventions like Tuesday's Child, we can see how the inverse may also be true—the strategy implemented to solve a problem in return shapes how we define it. By focusing the intervention at the family level, therapeutic and behavioral interventions inherently locate the problem there as well.

As we have seen in the previous chapters, young children's frustration and anger lead to physical aggression, and, according to the American Academy of Pediatrics, this is developmentally normal (Shelov et al., 2014). Prevalence rates of truly disordered disruptive behaviors are very low (e.g., between 1% and 3% in community samples). When normative behaviors are labeled as disruptive or challenging, even for insurance purposes, it can lead to unnecessary interventions, such as being tracked into special education programming, and have a lasting impact on children and families. Further still, as we have established already, these behaviors are not necessarily at the root of children's exclusion. Our systematic review of early childhood expulsion found minimal evidence of children's diagnosed disability or behavioral problems predicting exclusion. Instead, teachers' perceptions of the behavior, or their fear of being held responsible for the danger or damage a child caused, more consistently predicted expulsion (Zinsser et al., 2022).

In the face of pervasive and persistent exclusion, however, Tuesday's Child has found a way to help, and they are making a meaningful impact in the lives of hundreds of families. But with thousands of children being formally expelled and countless others being pushed out of care across the country, we need to look for more universal and scalable solutions that address competencies in the workforce and disrupt and dismantle the biases and disparities in discipline across subgroups.

One such possible scalable prevention mechanism is through the promotion of children's social and emotional competence via social and emotional learning (SEL) programming. SEL describes the process by which children learn skills critical to lifelong academic and social success, such as managing one's thoughts and feelings, and relationship skills like sharing and cooperating. Children make tremendous gains in these developmental processes in early childhood, and there is a substantial body of work demonstrating the benefits of supporting such development in educational settings (for meta-analytic review, see Durlak et al., 2011). Theoretical models such as the

Calm Classroom model of Tish Jennings and Marc Greenberg (2009) lead researchers to expect that by intentionally providing children with high-quality guidance and instruction around how to manage their feelings, make responsible choices, and resolve conflict, many of the challenging behaviors attributed to expulsion would be prevented. In many ways, expulsion is the antithesis of SEL; rather than building competencies and skills, a child is shown to the door.

The substantial evidence behind SEL interventions has led all 50 states to include it in their early learning standards for Head Starts and other public prekindergartens; additionally, many center-based care programs have adopted formal curriculum and SEL promotion programs such as Second Step, Preschool PATHs, and Al's Pals (for a review, see the CASEL SELect Guide, www.casel.org). Unfortunately, despite the national attention, access and training around SEL are still lagging, especially in early childhood education. SEL is rarely a focus of pre-service teacher preparation programs (Schonert-Reichl et al., 2015), and only 20% of early childhood providers reported receiving in-service training on how to support children's social-emotional growth (US DOE and DHHS, 2014). Children are developing social and emotional skills in the classroom, whether or not teachers are intentionally providing instruction. To ensure that the lessons learned are prosocial and positive, a preliminary step toward eradicating expulsion must be to ensure that all early childhood teachers know how to intentionally and proactively support this development.

It was within this landscape of high rates of exclusion and low rates of SEL training in early childhood that I sought funding to launch the Chicago area teachers' study through the National Academy of Education. I've reported some results from this study in prior chapters, but the original overarching hypothesis for the study was that, in the absence of other policies precluding expulsion, programs with more SEL resources would expel fewer kids. However, an analysis of these Chicago area teachers' data revealed that not *access to*, but *frequent use of* any available SEL resources was correlated with lower rates of exclusion. However, the association was fully mediated by teacher stress. That is, to the extent that implementing an SEL curriculum to support children's social and emotional skills decreased teachers' experience of stress in the classroom, expulsions were reduced. However, if adding a new curriculum or complicated resource increased teacher stress—even if the resource was meant to support positive child behavior—expulsions could be more frequent.

Given our understanding of how teacher stress impacts their in-classroom reactions (see Chapter 5), this makes sense. As Vivian Tseng and Edward Seidman (2007) argue in their systems framework for understanding social settings, we must do more than provide resources to change social processes (such as teacher-child interactions). Even the best curriculum cannot make up for other hardships that teachers face in the classroom. For example, I asked teachers in a focus group in 2012 what they needed to support children's SEL. To my surprise, one teacher quipped, "I need an adult-sized chair! My back is killing me." She explained that she found it very difficult to rise from the child-sized furniture to respond to children's needs. Rather than proactively responding to the first sign of kids squabbling in the block corner, the teacher admitted that she frequently raised her voice and called across the room to break up an escalating conflict. She knew this was not ideal, but felt hampered by her environment. Had this teacher been handed a new curriculum to implement, it likely would have stayed in the box on a shelf. There were more pressing needs inhibiting its implementation. Implementation science has shown us time and again that the well-being of the workforce is paramount. None of the promising solutions to the expulsion crisis mentioned in this chapter will do an ounce of good if our early childhood teachers are exhausted and leaving the workforce.

As I hope has been evident throughout this book, efforts to prevent or reduce early childhood exclusion must address multiple systemic failures and change social processes at multiple levels. SEL programming and curriculum may hold promise to prevent some expulsions, but in the absence of more systemic reforms, such investments will fall short. Thankfully, there are several promising multilevel approaches to prevention, but none has been extensively evaluated for its impact on expulsion to date. Still, I will present three promising and lauded approaches, each of which places emphasis on supporting the adults so that they can better promote children's learning and well-being.

Promising Solution #1: The Pyramid Model for Promoting Young Children's Social-Emotional Competence

The Pyramid Model aims to provide early educators with guidance on practices that can be implemented within early childhood programs to promote young children's social-emotional development and address challenging behavior. The Pyramid Model was developed beginning in 2001 by a consortium of research scholars providing technical assistance to the Office of Head Start in direct response to the problems identified in our Chicago Teacher study—the lack of coordination and systemic support to implement evidence-based SEL programming in early childhood settings.

Instead of boxed curricula, the Pyramid Model is a tiered framework for organizing practices including universal social-emotional promotion, practices for children who need targeted social-emotional supports, and individualized behavior-support practices for children with significant social skill deficits or persistent challenging behavior. These three tiers of intervention are arranged hierarchically, with more children receiving less intensive proactive instruction on social and emotional skills and direct services targeting a few higher-need cases, hence the imagery of a pyramid. Pyramid Model practices are based on research examining ways to develop effective instruction, support children's engagement, promote children's social skills and emotional competencies, and leverage assessment-based behavior support plans for children with severe and persistent behavior challenges.

These three tiers all sit on the foundation of an effective workforce with expertise in engaging families and cultural humility. Teachers trained in the Pyramid Model use family-centered, culturally responsive strategies and understand that cultural expectations will impact how behavior is perceived. At the core of the framework is the belief that high-quality supportive environments, combined with nurturing and responsive relationships among children, families, and programs, can mitigate the vast majority of perceived behavioral challenges in the classroom, thus reserving more intensive interventions for those who need it.

What Does the Evidence Say?

Studies have demonstrated that teachers' use of the Pyramid Model practices is associated with improvements in children's social skills and challenging behavior. In Colorado, demonstration sites that maintained high fidelity with the Model saw a 60%–75% reduction in the perception of children rated as "at risk" on the Ages and Stages Social-Emotional Scale. At the same time, programs implementing the Model scored higher on state ratings of program-level quality. A robust randomized control trial of the Pyramid

Model, led by Mary Louise Hemmeter from Vanderbilt University, has found small to moderate Pyramid training effects on child behavioral outcomes. Specifically, while teachers in the Pyramid condition rated children's behavior as less challenging at the follow-up time point than teachers in the control group, direct observations of the matched focal children in each group of classrooms were not significantly different. However, as we have seen throughout this book, in some instances, changing the perception of behavior may be just as powerful an intervention from the teachers' standpoint.

The tiered supports and focus on promoting children's competence and teacher confidence in the classroom have led many to suggest that the Pyramid Model could serve as a broad system-wide exclusion prevention intervention. Over 20 states have adopted the Pyramid Model in response to the 2014 joint policy statement by the U.S. Departments of Health & Human Services and Education, encouraging localities to consider implementing Positive Behavior Supports and Interventions (PBIS) frameworks, like the Pyramid Model, to address the inappropriate use of discipline practices. When PBIS programs are implemented in schools, evidence has shown that they can decrease the number of office referrals, especially for kindergarteners, and reduce (but not eliminate) the racial disparities in discipline (Bradshaw et al., 2010; Vincent et al., 2011). However, despite the enthusiasm and momentum around the Pyramid Model, there remains limited evidence that this program designed and implemented specifically in early childhood settings can similarly curtail disciplinary exclusion broadly or the racial disparities in discipline explicitly.

One study we can examine is a 2016 publication by Megan Vinh and Phil Strain at the Universities of North Carolina, Chapel Hill, and Colorado, Denver, respectively. Their analysis compared rates of exclusion from Colorado child-care programs in 2006 and 2011, bookending the 2009 passage of a policy initiative to implement the Pyramid Model statewide. Although these are not identical longitudinal samples, each survey drew on several hundred programs' responses and represented a broad array of funding streams and types (licensed home and center-based care, non- and for-profit, faith-based, and Head Start programs). Vihn and Strain report that rates of removal decreased substantially from 2006 to 2011. Specifically, in 2006, 10 children out of every 1,000 were suspended or expelled. That rate drops to 4 per 1,000 in 2011. Further, the vast majority of programs (84.1%) responding to the 2011 survey indicated that no child had been removed due to challenging behaviors that year.

More recently, Kelsey Clayback and M. L. Hemmeter (2021) published a correlational study of directors' reports of exclusionary discipline in over 300 child-care centers in Pennsylvania. This research team specifically asked directors to report on their programs' use of the Pyramid Model Strategies, which had recently been incorporated into the state's technical assistance offerings. Among other key findings related to the protective effect of directors' own job satisfaction and well-being, Clayback and Hemmeter found that center-wide use of the Pyramid Model strategies was associated with significantly fewer expulsions. The authors posit that the Pyramid Model may reduce exclusionary discipline by providing the support that teachers desperately need to prevent challenging behavior in the classroom, in addition to strategies of how best to respond when it does occur. Further, the Model's guidance of how to effectively communicate with families may help build mutually respectful and trusting relationships.

While we cannot imply causality from either of these studies, they show promise. At the same time, it is notable that there has not been a more direct evaluation of the Pyramid Model's impact on expulsion and suspension rates. One can hope that as states scale up their adoption and implementation of this evidence-based model to support child social-emotion development, they also continue to monitor and collect robust data on disciplinary actions taken by Pyramid Model programs to facilitate future evaluations.

Cashing in on the promise of the Pyramid Model as an expulsion-prevention tool will require that early childhood programs are fully implementing the model with high fidelity. Full implementation of the Pyramid Model entails establishing staff buy-in, engaging with families, establishing program-wide expectations, providing ongoing professional development and classroom coaching, establishing procedures for responding to the needs of children with challenging behavior, and using data to monitor implementation and outcomes (Fox et al., 2003; Hemmeter et al., 2007). Unfortunately, this is rarely achieved, especially in community-based settings. Research has demonstrated that, on average, teachers in community-based early childhood settings, *without training and support*, are implementing the Pyramid Model practices at about 40% fidelity (Hemmeter et al., 2018). To see meaningful impacts of the Model at the child level, teachers needed to receive training on the model and 16 weeks of individualized coaching. Even then, many teachers reported feeling challenged by the lack of support from school administrators and the lack of school supports for implementing tertiary interventions that required facilitation by a behavior specialist or a professional with behavioral expertise (Hemmeter et al., 2018). Some suggest that full implementation of program-wide efforts like the Pyramid Model would take multiple years of training and support. Given the high turnover rate in early childhood education settings, it is unclear if this is sustainable.

Like the Pyramid Model, multi-tiered culturally responsive interventions are precisely the direction we need to be heading when we think about building and maintaining a robust early childhood system. Regardless of how powerful the intervention is on paper, its impact will be diluted when added post hoc into a disjointed (and some may say dysfunctional) system that itself is couched within a society that undervalues young children and the people who care for and educate them.

Promising Solution #2: Infant and Early Childhood Mental Health Consultation

Infant and Early Childhood Mental Health Consultation (IECMHC) is the process by which an individual with expertise in infant and early childhood mental health collaborates with teachers, center directors, and families to build their capacities to support young children's healthy social-emotional development. Consultants are often social workers with additional credentials and can work as part of a statewide network of professionals who carry caseloads of centers or programs. In larger settings, consultants can also be dedicated to a specific program (e.g., a Head Start center). In many ways, the components of consultation have remained unchanged since its inclusion in the 1972 Head Start Program Performance Standards, but it is only recently that consultation has been held up as a promising prevention tool against early childhood expulsion. The recency of the connection was summed up by a consultant from Illinois Action for Children, Anne Konen, "Consultation has nothing but everything to do with preventing expulsion." We saw in Roseanne and Jiang's story in Chapter 7 how consultation can lead to impactful change for the child and program. Here we will look under the hood of consultation to understand how this intervention works and what barriers still exist.

Consultation is grounded in trusting relationships among the adults who care for young children. It is in the context of these long-lasting relationships that consultants provide teachers and practitioners with information and support around children's behavioral concerns. Annie Davis and colleagues at the Center for Excellence for Infant and Early Childhood Mental Health Consultation described how consultants and practitioners "wonder together about the child to understand his perspective better to consider contextual influences on behavior and to view the challenging behavior as an expression of a need" (Davis et al., 2020, p. 329). As teachers gain this perspective with the consultant's reflective support, they increase their opportunities to have positive interactions with the focal child and all children in the classroom. Over time, these positive interactions improve child and family outcomes and benefit teachers' sense of efficacy, job satisfaction, and well-being. In turn, these changes should improve the classroom climate and a broader positive feedback loop.

On the surface, consultation may seem simplistic. Those who have spent time working in early care and education settings can readily recall how rare it is to have time and space to engage in reflection and creative problem-solving. Preschool classrooms are busy, noisy, and joyful places, but teachers must always be on alert, anticipating the needs of 18 busy little bodies. Who needs an extra warning before the next transition? When is Suzie's mom coming to get her to go to the dentist? Where else can we look for Josh's mitten? Especially in under-staffed settings, like those that Lance and Nathan attended, teachers barely have time to take a bathroom break, let alone analyze their capacity to provide individualized, culturally responsive care or advocate for needed supports and resources. Consultants create that space for teachers to take a breath, express their subjective experiences free of judgment, and question their own choices, perceptions, and reactions. The primary mechanism in consultation has sometimes been called "inquiry as an intervention"—that is, practice changes because there is a protected space (physically, temporally, and psychologically) for teachers to reflect on their practice. The belief in self-reflection is so deeply embedded that it has been called "early childhood's superpower."[1]

[1] This phrase was used by Dr. Cynthia Tate, the former director of the Illinois Governor's Office of Early Childhood, when accepting an achievement award from the Illinois Association of Infant Mental Health on October 29, 2020.

Potential to Interrupt Bias

In their 2020 conceptual model of IECMHC, Annie Davis, Deborah Perry, and Lauren Rabinovitz argue that there are many similarities between consultation and existing implicit bias interventions. For example, Okonofua's intervention (see Chapter 7) challenged middle-school teachers to consider how the environment influences their students' behavior and emphasized positive relationships. Similar themes are at the core of consultation and discussions of race and gender bias are common in the consultative process. For example, consultants may ask teachers to consider how their own cultural beliefs and experiences impact their reactions to a child or a child's parents. Such nonjudgmental "wonderings" are expected to help the teacher develop greater self-awareness and empathy, which supports communication with families. At the same time, Davis and colleagues warn that if the relationship between the consultant and teacher is weak, such as when consultation is only a short-term intervention, such open wondering about sensitive topics like race could backfire as teachers feel criticized and defensive.

When done well, consultation holds promise for reducing teachers' automatic associations or implicit biases based on children's identities. One respondent interviewed by Davis said, "implicit bias is the opposite of the stance of curiosity" (2020, p. 335). To the extent that consultation can create space for teachers' natural curiosity about their practice and individual children's unique needs, it may indeed be our best hope for reducing disparities. For now, these pathways are still theoretical. To date, no studies have explicitly tested the impact of consultation on teachers' implicit biases. There is some evidence, however, that consultants with expertise in cultural diversity may be better able to develop strong consultative alliances with teachers, a key component of the theoretical model to reduce expulsions (Davis et al., 2018).

What Does the Evidence Say?

Numerous state-agency reports and evaluations have demonstrated the significant and positive impacts of infant and early childhood consultation across multiple levels. The Healthy Futures project (2014) evaluated four years of data from Washington, D.C.'s consultation model across 25 child-care centers in low-income neighborhoods across the city. Teachers who received consultation scored significantly higher on measures of teacher-child interactions compared to baseline. They were more positive, less punitive, and less detached. Likewise, teachers and parents reported that focal children's behavior was significantly less concerning, and teachers rated children as having higher self-regulation, initiative, and attachment after engaging with a consultant. Dr. John Carlson and colleagues also reported positive impacts of the Michigan consultation model in 2012. Over the course of a 6-month window, 44 consultants worked with 432 child-family cases. Parents and teachers both reported that, with targeted consultation, children became less hyperactive and showed improvements in their social skills. Child-care providers also reported a greater sense of competence in managing children's behavior after working with consultants. Finally, a 2016 report on the Pennsylvania Early Childhood Mental Health Consultation Project summarized 2 years of program data. Consultants served 680 children by working with their teacher(s), parents, and program directors across 400 child-care centers. Findings included significant improvements in teachers' reports of children's behavior and implementation of recommended social-emotional strategies, and decreases in teacher-reported stress.

Consultation is a well-regarded means of supporting and enhancing our nation's fragile early childhood education system's capacity. It also acts on many of the levers related to exclusionary discipline discussed so far, including teachers' efficacy and confidence in the classroom, perceptions of children's behavior, and teacher-child relationships. Some studies and evaluations have also indicated that consultation can result in lower teacher-reported stress (e.g., Davis & Perry, 2016), but this association is not consistent across studies (likely due to variations in measurement and use of unvalidated scales; Gilliam, 2007). The generally positive results attributed to consultation have led to it being lauded among policymakers as our best hope for reducing expulsions. Indeed, there is some evidence that consultation services prevent or reduce the risk of children being excluded, but the existing evidence base is relatively small. While the theory of change is clear, more research is needed to cultivate empirical evidence of each mechanism and pathway.

In his 2005 analysis of the national prekindergarten study data, Walter Gilliam tested whether access to an infant and early childhood mental health consultant was associated with the use of exclusionary discipline. This cross-sectional study was the first and most widely cited evidence of the positive impact of consultation on expulsion practices. Of the nearly 4,000 classrooms responding from across the country, Gilliam found that those with no access to consultation services expelled nearly twice as many children (10.76 per 1,000) as programs with a consultant onsite or one who made regular visits (5.68 per 1,000). Programs that had a consultant on call also expelled fewer children, but slightly more than when one was onsite (6.17 per 1,000).

The other most commonly cited evidence of consultation as an expulsion-prevention strategy comes from a mixed-method study by Deborah Perry (Perry et al., 2008). As part of a 4-year-long evaluation of Maryland's statewide consultation system, researchers followed the experiences of nearly 200 children at risk of being expelled from their child-care programs. Identified children received individualized consultation, and the vast majority were rated more positively by their providers over time and were retained by their centers. Only 13 children left their placements involuntarily. The evaluators interviewed the consultant who was working with the excluding program, the program's director, and the child's parents to understand the factors that led to the expulsions and the role of the consultant. Perry's interviews were in line with the conceptual model described above. Consultants aimed to build capacity by promoting positive adult-to-adult interactions (teacher-teacher, teacher-director, teacher/director-parent, etc.). This qualitative study included examples of program-level and child-specific strategies employed by consultants trying to forestall a child's exclusion. Programmatic strategies included changes to the classroom routine to reduce a child's idle waiting during transitions and the addition of social-emotional learning materials. For focal children, consultants recommended sensory techniques (e.g., wiggle cushions to sit on during circle time), using visual timers to help a child anticipate a transition, or empowering a child with a special job role (e.g., line leader) to build responsibility and prevent disruption.

More recently, the Yale Child Study Center team, including Walter Gilliam, Angela Maupin, and Chin Reyes, published one of the most rigorous evaluations to date. Results of their statewide evaluation of the Connecticut consultation system were published in a 2016 volume of *Journal of the American Academy of Child & Adolescent Psychiatry.* Two target children from each of 88 preschool classrooms across the state were identified as at risk of expulsion and were randomly assigned to either receive consultation or be placed on a wait-list for treatment. At the end of the 12-week intervention, children who received consultations were rated as less hyperactive and restless and displaying fewer problem behaviors than control group children.

However, the intervention did not significantly impact the classroom environment, nor did it affect the likelihood of a child being expelled.

Taken together, these three studies paint an optimistic but still blurry picture about consultation. Given the relative infrequency of expulsion and the challenges associated with measuring other forms of exclusion, continued work to develop and validate expulsion-risk measures may be fruitful. Although Gilliam's preschool expulsion-risk measure did not predict exclusion in the Connecticut study, scores significantly decreased in a cross-sectional sample from Alameda County, California, in a report by Eva Marie Shiver and colleagues (2019).

Beyond measurement, however, other significant challenges and barriers limit the scope and impact of consultation, including access, response times, and turnover. Readers looking to see examples of robust state-level implementation of consultation models could turn to several examples, including Arizona, Connecticut, Pennsylvania, and Ohio. However, state level is not the same as statewide. In Pennsylvania, for example, early childhood programs were only eligible to receive consultation services if they were already participating in the state's quality rating improvement system (Keystone STARS). According to an external evaluation in 2016, these criteria limited the reach of the intervention. Programs that were most likely to need help ending exclusionary discipline practices—those in rural and under-resourced communities and lower-quality and non-center-based care providers—were generally excluded from consultation services.

In other states, such as Illinois, even though these types of programs theoretically have access to consultation, the wait times preclude their participation. Administrators participating in our 2018 study reported a wait time of 3–4 months before a consultant could visit their center. There is only one consultant per county in many parts of the state, and they must drive several hours to reach a center in crisis. The consultation service model typically relies on a program to self-identify as needing assistance and reaching out for help. Consultants complain that programs initiate this process too late, when they are already on the verge of expelling a child. Developing good rapport and igniting the teacher's curiosity and self-reflection are nearly impossible when a teacher is already at the end of her rope with an individual child. Finally, regardless of how a state administers consultation or how many weeks of observations and reflection a center receives, high staff turnover rates can eradicate progress overnight.

Promising Solution #3: Arkansas' BehaviorHelp System

Our third and final promising solution is, in many ways, a combination of the first two. Arkansas's statewide expulsion-prevention system for early childhood programs coordinates tiers of supports to providers across the state. Just as in the Pyramid Model, the BehaviorHelp system was designed based on the premise that most challenging behavior can be addressed by supporting teachers to engage in the practices that support positive relationships and build children's social and emotional skills. A smaller proportion of children's behavior will require more intensive intervention where a clinical lens could be beneficial.

In Arkansas, when a program or provider reaches out to the BehaviorHelp system, a specialist interviews them to understand the nature of the problem and then refers them to one of three tiers of support. The program was designed so that most programs should have their needs met by working with a specialist over the phone or via email (Tier 1). A smaller number of programs receive short-term technical assistance over a handful of visits and observations (Tier 2). Assistance provided at this second tier focuses on helping teachers implement social-emotional teaching practices and reducing behavior concerns by strengthening the classroom environment's overall quality. Programs can also receive recommendations and referrals for additional tailored professional development needs. Finally, the minority of programs require onsite infant and early childhood mental health consultation (Tier 3). As in other consultation models discussed above, this third tier entails 12–16 weeks of an intensive collaboration between the consultant, program staff, and families, including observations, training, reflective supervision, and referrals to community resources.

In a 2020 paper summarizing a 3-year evaluation of the BehaviorHelp system, Nicola Conners Edge at the University of Arkansas and collaborators from key state agencies reported significant short- and long-term outcomes. BehaviorHelp team members rated programs as highly engaged and receptive to support. For those receiving consultation (Tier 3), results showed that the BehaviorHelp approach had similarly positive impacts on children's behavior and hyperactivity. Although a larger proportion of programs needed Tier 2 supports than initially anticipated, that assistance paid off. Of the over 1,100 cases referred to BehaviorHelp, only 32 children were expelled (2.9%). Two-thirds of children stayed in the center that initially requested help, and the vast majority of these even stayed in the same classroom. The remaining cases closed when a program closed, a child entered kindergarten, or the parents moved away.

In their discussion of the results, the researchers conclude that this multi-tiered approach fits what we know about the various and complex pathways toward exclusion. While most exclusions can be triggered by a teachers' lack of knowledge, skill, or resources, some may also require more targeted support around the special education or mental health needs of a child. Expulsion-prevention strategies must adjust to provide the right kind of support to programs and families. A classroom may appear chaotic, and children's behavior seems erratic when there is no predictable routine, or the materials are not engaging or developmentally appropriate. In this case, technical assistance may be much more fruitful than intensive consultation. Simultaneously, resources for the classroom and general training may not be sufficient to help a teacher persist and collaborate with the family of a child who had experienced complex trauma.

Regardless of the teachers' and children's underlying needs, the call for action is growing louder, and our collective inaction has ripple effects. When left unsupported, teachers burn out and quit, leaving a vacuum that is difficult to fill with a qualified and competent candidate. When left unaddressed, a child's behavior and reputation follow them into elementary school, leaving kindergarten teachers and families frustrated and ill-prepared to help. When left unaddressed, we as a country continue to disproportionately and harshly punish Black children's behavior, placing them on the preschool-to-prison pipeline before they can even read.

Throughout this book, I have tried to introduce the reader to the numerous and interrelated factors that contribute to our nation's exclusion of children from early childhood programs. While we do not know everything, and evidence of causal pathways is still accumulating, it should be evident that combating this national crisis cannot happen at the program level. It is going to take coordinated systemic change, driven by inclusive public policy. Single centers or programs may have success retaining and adequately supporting children, but wide-scale change cannot happen ad hoc. Therefore, we will turn our attention to the legislative and policy efforts being implemented across the country, their relative scope, and preliminary evidence of impact.

9

Pulling Policy Levers to Curtail Expulsion

Aiden (pseudonym) was about to turn 4 when he was expelled from his first program. Blossom Day Care Center (pseudonym) was in a suburb of Chicago just west of O'Hare airport. One of a handful of programs on the main road, Blossom was a relatively small private program with one room each for infants and toddlers and two pre-K classes. They also offered before- and after-school care with kids arriving on a bus from the elementary program. Aiden's mom, Lydia (pseudonym), initially chose the program because it was on her route to work and offered flexible enough hours to accommodate her occasional overtime schedule. The strip mall storefront backed up to a park, and the children had frequent opportunities to play outside, weather permitting.

Early in 2018, Aiden moved into the older classroom. In this more structured environment, he struggled to pay attention, transition, and follow instructions. "At first, I thought it was just that he missed his old teacher, but then he started to complain and . . . didn't want to go anymore." Leaving the house in the morning started becoming a battle, "He would have tantrums, kick, scream, throw things, and he even started biting again." The school started seeing the same behaviors in the classroom. One particular trigger for Aiden was the program's napping policy. Aiden had stopped napping long ago, but the expectation in this classroom was that children stay on their cots for the 2-hour nap time. "Yeah, right," his mom said, "you try to tell a [little kid] to stay anywhere longer than 5 minutes quietly!"

Very rapidly, the center started showing signs that they couldn't work with Aiden. "I would be called by the director several times a week . . . to come to pick him up." After leaving work early multiple times in a single week, she finally said, "I've had enough . . . I can't keep coming here and leaving work," but the director didn't offer any help. Desperate and feeling alone, Aiden's mom took him to be evaluated by a private practice occupational therapist (OT) in the city. He was quickly diagnosed with oral sensory issues, which explained the biting. The OT recommended a therapist who came to observe the classroom and offered recommendations to the teachers, but nothing changed. The director made it clear that Aiden wasn't welcome at the center, and it seemed from his protests to go every morning that he knew it. Lydia began searching for another program.

Lydia found a slot for Aiden at Peggy's Playschool (pseudonym), another private program about 20 minutes away. The added drive time meant Lydia had to wake him earlier, but she hoped that the program's play-based approach would better suit his learning needs. Very quickly, though, the same behaviors started cropping up: "he would spit, hit, kick, scream, and bite. One of the teachers even admitted to me that she slapped him on the hand after he hit her. I was livid," his mother shared.

She started bringing him to a child psychologist, but his behavior didn't change quickly enough. Within weeks of his enrollment, the Playschool director was encouraging her to get Aiden evaluated for the special education program at the public school. Knowing that the public program was only a part-day program, Lydia instead sought guidance from her pediatrician. The doctor wrote a referral to Easter Seals, an early intervention and family support services non-profit in Illinois. When Lydia emailed the director to tell her that the Easter Seals therapist would like to work with Aiden at the school, the director called her back, saying that she would not allow a therapist in her facility and further that "other parents are complaining [about Aiden] and she wants him out of her program."

The staff at Easter Seals had given Lydia information about a new law in Illinois. It was now technically illegal for the program to expel Aiden because of his behavior. But when Lydia emailed the information sheet to the Playschool director and explained that she could not legally kick Aiden out, "she replied she had never heard of that, and she has the right to kick out whoever [sic] she wants to." Lydia's next step was to call the Department of Children and Family Services and report the Playschool. "Within two days, the licensing representative was at the facility, and the director changed her tune. I got a call from his teacher saying that the therapist could come work with Aiden now. But at that point . . . I was too angry." She knew this wasn't a place for her child. The teachers and director and other families had made their mind up about him, and even though they were no longer directly telling her he was expelled, she certainly felt like she was being shown the door.

While she was actively searching for a new care arrangement, she called one afternoon to check on Aiden. The director told her, "he was being terrible," so I left work and went during nap time to pick him up, "he was crying and so upset he was hyper-ventilating . . . no one was helping him. . . . I just scooped him up and held him tight and calmed him right there in front of all of [the staff]."

"They treated him like he was some heathen. It was horrible. So I took him out of there and never brought him back. I had to advocate for my son. No one helped me. No one knew anything about any resources."

With two expulsions in a matter of months, Lydia and Aiden were both exhausted. She began trying to get him enrolled in the school district Pre-K program, where they would be required to provide him with an evaluation and an Individualized Education Plan (IEP) if warranted. Unfortunately, as is typical in most districts, this program was only part-time, and so Lydia also had to find extended-hour care within the school district's busing radius.

Her choices were minimal, and in the end, there was only one with an opening that the bus would go to. Over the barrel, Lydia paid the deposit but was reticent, "it was dirty and old and run down. The teachers seemed so unhappy to be there, but it was the only option. But the problems there continued too. The hitting, biting, pushing. The usual."

"It being the 3rd daycare, I knew he just couldn't do that environment. The loud noises, too many people, too much structure. [It was causing] him too much anxiety, and he acts out. He was only there for three and a half weeks before I got a nanny."

Ironically, this program was very willing to work with Lydia. They welcomed the occupational therapist and other specialists who needed to evaluate him for the public school program. "But almost every day, I had a [incident] report. Kids would bother him, get in his face . . . and he would bite someone or hit or push."

At the time of Lydia's interview, Aiden was making real progress. He spent the early morning and afternoons with a nanny and one other child, a young toddler. From nine to noon each day, he attended the school district's special education program, where he had a one-on-one aide and an IEP. Recently, he was diagnosed with a sensory processing disorder, which helped explain his intense reactions to the other children. Lydia and the nanny were learning from his teachers how to support Aiden's interactions. "He's doing amazingly. Not one issue at home or at school."

As exhausting as Lydia's experience had been, she retained some perspective, "Daycares in the U.S. are severely understaffed, and our licensing requirements are just setting those poor teachers up for failure." She empathized with the directors who are just trying to run their business. Still, at the same time, she felt like she should not be the only one looking out for her child's interests and doing all of the legwork trying to find solutions; "as parents, we put our trust in the hands of these centers. We trust that they will treat our children with respect, care, and compassion. So, in my opinion, they should be the ones that are knowledgeable in this area and offer supports to parents. There was zero compassion, no offer to help, nothing. Just 'get him out of here.' 'He's not normal.' It broke my heart."

* * *

At this point, a story like this should feel too familiar—a family is in a tailspin following a series of exclusions and formal expulsions. The existing supports and safety nets do not meet their needs and become available only after multiple negative experiences. Perhaps the real difference between this and previous stories highlighted in this book is timing. Technically, Aiden could not be formally expelled because of the passage of a unique law in Illinois just a few months prior. Unfortunately, as Lydia discovered, even the explicit rules and regulations banning expulsion cannot end the practices alone. Implementing such policies takes a great deal more than a governor's signature. As we have seen throughout this book, expulsions wreak havoc on children and families, but they are also symptomatic of a broken system of early care and education. Abolishing the practice requires that we shine a light on the shortcomings and under-investment in that system. Further, implementing any large-scale systemic reform will require coordination among policymakers, advocates, practitioners, and funding streams.

I am by no means a policy expert. However, as a community-based researcher, I have continually looked upward in the care system, following the empirical evidence up from the classroom level. I have spent the last several years trying to understand how, when, and where policy plays a role in the expulsion process. In this chapter, I will use the story of our ongoing evaluation of the Illinois expulsion law to examine what it takes to craft, pass, and implement early childhood expulsion policy. In addition to discovering the law's impact, this case study will also illuminate the potential pitfalls and continued challenges along the way. But before we can dive in, it is important to understand the broader federal and state policy landscape and the different approaches employed across the country.

As of this writing, the United States is still reeling from the tumultuous 2020 election and the only partially abated spread of COVID-19. Both immensely historical events will have long-lasting impacts on nearly every facet of our lives, including the regulation of child care and early learning in our nation. Specific to discipline policies, however, this period feels like one of transition. Federal policy and guidelines around school discipline have swung to extremes under the prior two administrations, and advocates are hopeful that we have not lost momentum on the issue. Simultaneously, the already stressed early childhood systems are buckling under public health–mandated closures and enrollment caps, skyrocketing cleaning and protective equipment costs, and a workforce that is more susceptible to the disease because of inadequate compensation and benefits, structural racism, and inequality.

We can trace policymakers' involvement in school discipline to the 1980s and 1990s. A rise in school violence and shootings put pressure on administrators to aggressively respond to misbehavior (Stinchcomb et al., 2006) and increase the police presence in schools (Welch & Payne, 2010). Policymakers encouraged schools to implement rigid disciplinary codes (e.g., zero-tolerance and three-strikes policies), despite zero evidence that such approaches were effective deterrents (American Psychological Association, 2008; American Academy of Pediatrics, 2013). Unfortunately, although White offenders primarily perpetuated the school shootings, these crackdowns disproportionately and negatively impacted Black and Brown students. Racial disparities in suspensions and expulsion have been evident since the U.S. Department of Education's Office for Civil Rights (OCR) began collecting data on student demographics in the 1960s. Still, the increased police presence opened the floodgates of the school-to-prison pipeline.

In response to increasing evidence of persistent racial disparities, the U.S. Department of Justice and the OCR issued joint school-discipline guidelines in 2014. Under the Obama administration, the OCR was particularly concerned with understanding and preventing these disparities. Guidelines included examples of ways discrimination can occur and a list of potential evidence-based remedies, including restorative and school-wide approaches to improving school climate and reducing misbehavior. The guidelines also outlined a legal framework for assessing racial discrimination allegations, which is critical to systemic reform (Lewis et al., 2019). Notably, this coincided with the first OCR report to include data from public preschools, which we discussed in Chapter 2, prompting this joint guidance to apply to pre-K through 12th grade. It was the first national effort to acknowledge and address the early childhood discipline crisis.

Later that same year, the U.S. Departments of Health and Human Services and Education released a joint policy statement calling states to establish policies to broadly abolish exclusionary discipline in early childhood settings. This recommendation became more salient when members of the Congressional Black Caucus[1] successfully lobbied to require states to report on their early childhood suspension and expulsion policies as a condition of receiving support child care for low-income working families through the Child Care & Development Block Grant (CCDBG).

Soon after, Head Start, the nation's largest federally funded early childhood program, clarified its firm stance on the issue in their updated performance standards (U.S. Department of Health and Human Services, 2016). In 2016 the Office of Child Care issued guidance that included recommendations such as: (a) developing and implementing fair and appropriate policies that limit exclusionary discipline which are then applied without bias; (b) supporting the development of a highly skilled workforce, by striving to build capacity in the workforce to promote social and emotional development, prevent and manage challenging behavior, and understand culture; (c) increasing access to specialized supports with the aim that all providers have access to early childhood mental health consultants and/or behavior coaches; (d) strengthening family partnerships, especially around strategies to promote social and emotional development and collaborate early to address behavior concerns; (e) implementing universal screenings to ensure early identification and services; and (f) tracking data around rates of and disparities in suspension and expulsion in early childhood education settings.

Despite this momentum, just a few short months later, the political will to shine a light on the exclusionary discipline crisis seemingly evaporated. The Trump administration rescinded the Obama-era discipline guidance and proposed significant reductions to the budget and scope of the Civil Rights Data Collection effort. Although this was later overturned in court and Congress ultimately increased the budget of the OCR, under Secretary of Education Betsy Devos, efforts to understand and interrupt systemic issues and biases in education ground to a halt.

As this book moves to production, we are still awaiting the Senate vote on President Biden's Build Back Better human infrastructure bill. With

[1] One of the most influential voices on the caucus that year was my own representative, Danny K. Davis of the Illinois 7th district. I had the honor of meeting Representative Davis a few years later when my 2-year-old son and I visited the Hill with Zero to Three's "Strolling Thunder" advocacy event. As he let my son drive toy cars across his coffee table and try on his Chicago Bears helmet, I had the rare experience of talking about the intersection of my research and my community with someone in a position of power.

provisions including paid family leave, tax credits, universal pre-K, and increased compensation of early childhood professionals, this bill's passage would mark one of the largest reinvestments in children and families in generations (Guarino, 2021). However, this change in federal priorities is occurring during the most significant public health crisis in over 100 years. The COVID-19 pandemic has decimated the nation's early care and education system. According to an analysis by the Center for American Progress (2020), nearly 4.5 million child-care slots could be lost as upwards of 30% of programs nationwide permanently shutter during the pandemic. Simultaneously, the restrictions on enrollment and closure of programs and schools to reduce the spread of the coronavirus have sharply reminded working families and employers how dependent our economy is on a functional, safe, and high-quality system of care for children ages birth to 5.

A post-COVID child-care system may be ripe for a spike in exclusionary discipline. Providers under financial strain and anxious about their own health as frontline workers will undoubtedly experience high stress levels. Children who return to child care have accrued experience likely to strain their developing behavioral control skills—social isolation, housing and food insecurity, and grief. Nearly 140,000 children in the United States lost a primary or secondary caregiver from COVID as of October 2021. Even those not directly impacted by the virus will experience indirect losses. Parents, kept socially distant and barred from entering buildings for drop-off and pick-up, will have few if any opportunities to get to know their children's teachers. Those programs that managed to remain open will likely have long wait-lists full of desperate working families eager to take the spot of a child whose behavior is just too challenging.

This health crisis may have exacerbated many of the pathways to exclusionary discipline that we have discussed thus far. Even with federal leadership and reinvestment, it is unlikely that those pathways will vanish entirely. As was recently reiterated in a comprehensive report by the Children's Equity Project, while "federal recommendations influence local action, it is states, local districts, and early childhood programs that have ownership over discipline policies" (2020, p. 49). This is because states and localities decide how best to spend federal flow-through dollars from block grants for child care and preschool. At the state level, reimbursement and licensing requirements can motivate programs to implement new policies and practices or to meet specified targets. For many, the 2014 block grant served as an impetus to begin developing policies to prevent expulsion. Now, nearly a decade later, there is uneven progress being made across the nation.

To comply with the federal guidelines and stipulations, states across the country are trying to limit the expulsion of young children from preschool and early learning programs using various administrative and legislative actions and with varying success (Grossman-Kahn et al., 2018). According to an ongoing scan of policies in 40 states and the District of Colombia (Smith & McCann, 2020), only 19 states require providers to develop program-level discipline policies. Fourteen require that providers use supports such as mental health consultation, but only 11 require providers to create behavior plans for children at risk of being expelled. Thirteen states stipulate requirements that providers report program data related to expulsions and suspensions or resources programs have used, but only five require them to support families who are transitioning to a more suitable care arrangement.

Some states, such as Colorado and Louisiana, denounce exclusionary discipline in published administrative guides, reporting standards, and reimbursement requirements. Like Arkansas, others are enacting systemic reforms in conjunction with broader support systems (see Chapter 8; Conners Edge et al., 2018, 2020). At least 19 states have successfully passed legislation on the issue (Davis et al., 2020; Meek et al., 2020). Yet, states vary in the breadth of their efforts, with many policies applying to only certain age-bands, funding types, or program types (e.g., only children enrolled in public-school-based prekindergarten). Each approach has strengths and weaknesses. Administrative actions, such as memos and advisory statements to providers, are relatively easy to implement but have no real accountability mechanisms. Conversely, tying prohibitions to reimbursement is more likely to change program practices. Still, it will only influence programs that receive those funds (e.g., public prekindergarten, or voucher reimbursements for low-income families) and could require a significant investment in human resources and data systems to assess compliance.

At the local level, school districts such as Baltimore, Philadelphia, Los Angeles, and Chicago have imposed restrictions on exclusionary discipline for their youngest students (e.g., Grossman-Kahn et al., 2018). In Chicago, these restrictions came in the form of a 2014 revision to the student code of conduct that prohibits the use of suspensions for children enrolled in the pre-K through 2nd grades (expulsions for this age group had already been banned). The code of conduct only applies to students attending Chicago public schools, a small proportion of the total early childhood population, but had immediate and drastic effects. To facilitate the prohibition, the district also implemented supports and resources, including multi-tier systems of support (a K–12 equivalent of the Pyramid Model discussed in Chapter 8). The district restructured its data systems to allow for better tracking of behavior and intervention data. The district also hired more social-emotional specialists who served as consultants and coaches for schools struggling to manage a child's behavioral needs. Social-emotional learning routines, including standardized morning meetings at the classroom level, helped children develop concrete skills. The effects were immediate. Zero prekindergartners were suspended from Chicago public schools the following year.

In Colorado, policymakers used updating the state's child-care rules as an opportunity to comply with the CCDBG stipulations. The 2015 rule change affected more than 4,500 child-care centers statewide. The new rules included minimum hours of social-emotional professional development that providers had to complete, requirements around how programs document and outline their disciplinary decisions, and the requirement that programs implement SEL and family-engagement programming. To facilitate these new rules, 2019 legislation required the state to expand its professional development offerings and supports for the early childhood workforce and to double the mental health consultation workforce (a significant financial investment that received unanimous support from state legislators). Colorado also codified its model of consultation to set common job qualifications and expectations across the state to ensure equitable service delivery and experiences.

Spotlight on Illinois

As we've seen above, the ways that jurisdictions can approach the expulsion crisis are many and varied. Each has emerged from a unique context, a specific political climate, and a nuanced early childhood funding system. To better understand how these issues come together to influence what gets passed and how it works, we'll next dive more deeply into a single state's efforts: Illinois.

On August 14, 2017, Illinois Governor Bruce Rauner signed into law House Bill 2663, legislation aimed at ending the practice of expelling infants, toddlers, and preschoolers from their early childhood programs. The new law, Public Act (PA) 100-0105, represents the culmination of a multi-year collaborative effort by advocates, practitioners, parents, and policymakers. I was fortunate to be connected with some of these stakeholders in the fall of 2017. Chief among these new colleagues was Allison Lowe-Fotos, a policy manager at the Ounce of Prevention Fund (now called Start Early). When we met, Lowe-Fotos had already been part of a group advocating to get PA 100-0105 on the governor's desk for 2 years, and she quickly became my guide through the tangled early childhood policy landscape.

Advocates from across the state, representing the full spectrum of early childhood practitioners, services, and agencies, were pushing for sweeping reform, not locally isolated efforts to prevent expulsion. They wanted to ensure similar protections for children in a range of early learning programs, regardless of location, population served, or funding. The language of the bill was carefully revised over 18 months as the advocates met with stakeholders at every level: parents, providers, legislative staff, state agencies, justice groups, and public-school officials. This long revision process had two primary benefits. First, it significantly strengthened the bill's language. Second, by actively listening to and addressing multiple stakeholders' concerns, the team accumulated a long list of supporters, ultimately ensuring strong champions for the bill among legislators in Springfield. Key to the bill's success was the team's effort to prevent agency-level opposition by welcoming multiple stakeholders (namely the Board of Education and the Department of Children and Family Services) to be part of the process from the beginning. In the end, the bill was brought forward with strong bipartisan support and passed in a near-unanimous vote in the Senate.

Across both the state's school code and child-care act, Illinois PA 100-0105 explicitly called out the harmful and disproportionate effects of expulsion, stating, "Due to evidence that expulsion practices in the preschool years are linked to poor child outcomes and are employed inconsistently across racial and gender groups, early childhood programs . . . shall prohibit expulsions." However, the law went on to clarify that "[p]lanned transitions to settings that are able to better meet a child's needs are not considered expulsion." This stipulation was critical to gaining provider buy-in. Program and workforce advocates were concerned that an outright ban would leave providers liable if a staff member or another child became injured. Allowing for transitions was also considered developmentally appropriate practice, but as we'll see later on, it is a loophole that is difficult to define and close.

By amending both the school code *and* child care act, Illinois PA 100-0105 became the most comprehensive early childhood expulsion legislation to date. The Illinois expulsion law seeks to limit, if not end, the use of exclusionary discipline in any publicly funded or state-licensed early childhood program serving children between the ages of birth and 5 years. This includes public school prekindergarten, community-based child-care centers (publicly funded and tuition-based), and home-based family child care. Importantly, 100-0105 is also not tied to any single funding source. In some states, expulsion restrictions are tied to child-care assistance program voucher funding and therefore do not apply to most private programs. Instead, Illinois chose to tie this law to funding and licensing. Thus, across the thousands of providers across the state, only a handful of license-exempt programs do not have to comply (e.g., faith-based programs). It is the most inclusive and sweeping legislation to date. Uniquely, the Illinois law calls for coordination between the two state agencies that oversee nearly all early childhood programming in the state: the Illinois State Board of Education (ISBE) and the Illinois Department of Children and Family Services (DCFS). When the law went into effect in January 2018, these agencies were charged with co-writing rules and coordinating accountability systems.

To work across multiple types of programs, the IL expulsion law was written in broad language, with the intention that specific guidance would be developed in coordinated agency administrative rules. Additional requirements under the law included documentation, exhausting available resources and supports (including infant and early childhood mental health consultation), increasing training for teachers (including on topics such as implicit bias), and broad guidelines around planning transitions to more suitable care.

The law also stipulated that all programs would be required to report key data points to the state's education board. These data would include the size and demographic characteristics of their student body and the number of planned transitions and temporary removals disaggregated by race, gender, and disability status. Programs were also expected to report the total number of hours of consultation they received. Unfortunately, at the time and as of this writing, nearly 4 years after the law's passage, the state has no coordinated data system that would facilitate such a reporting process, nor a portal into which programs could enter such data.

Despite the bipartisan support for the law, it was passed during a state budget impasse. As such, there was also no funding allocated to increase supports to programs, disseminate information, or evaluate the law's impact. Without funding to develop the data-reporting portal, there were also no mechanisms that would allow policymakers to estimate expulsion rates or compliance across delivery systems. Nevertheless, the passage of IL 100-0105 was a monumental accomplishment for policymakers and advocates. This progressive, inclusive law stands out and could serve as a model for other states to implement broad reforms. Further, at the time, it was the only state to specify the need for implicit bias training while also requiring data to be reported in a disaggregated fashion, ostensibly allowing for evaluation (Davis et al., 2020).

After some brief back-slapping and celebration, the same advocates who fought for nearly 2 years to get the law passed knew that if they let up the pressure, this sweeping macro-policy effort would wither on the vine. As an unfunded mandate spreading across multiple state agencies that historically do not collaborate, there was a great deal of anxiety that the law would not be implemented as planned and would have limited effects. The advocates then shifted their focus to increasing resources to programs, staff, children, and families and supporting the joint rule-writing process. Beginning in the spring of 2018, the ISBE, the DCFS, and the Illinois Department of Human Services started working collaboratively with the Governor's Office of Early Childhood Development (GOECD) to develop rules, guidance, and best practices. However, after several months of joint meetings, the two agencies resumed working independently. The advocates who had initially fought hard to have these critical agencies collaborate and enact parallel rules were disheartened but not entirely surprised. There is a reason that multi-agency policy is rare. In this particular case, turnover in administrations and staffing and challenges associated with meeting each system's funding and legal requirements made the talks disjointed and difficult to sustain over time. ISBE, which had gone through similar rule-writing processes for their K–12 discipline policy changes several years prior, had the advantage and issued its rules in the spring of 2019. DCFS approved theirs the following fall. While there is overlap in the final rules, there are also substantial differences, even in definitions of what constitutes a behavior-support plan or a program-transition plan.

Through conversations with Lowe-Fotos, I became aware of the state's lack of funding and capacity to evaluate the legislation's impact. In the fall of 2017, after the law's passage but before it went into effect, we began meeting to discuss the rapid development of a survey to collect baseline expulsion rates from programs across the state. With funding from my university's social science research office and the Society for Community Research and Action, I began developing survey items in collaboration with stakeholders. A draft survey was shared with staff at the GOECD and members of the interagency task force charged with coordinating the new law's implementation. In early conversations, it was clear that there were three main issues concerning advocates and policymakers: the lack of baseline data against which to compare later assessments of expulsion, or infrastructure to collect such data statewide; that providers were ill-informed and unprepared to comply with the law; and that there may be significant unintended consequences, such as programs refusing to admit individual children for fear they would later display challenging behaviors.

To ensure that this study's findings were meaningful to those most likely to utilize them, my research team convened a coalition of early childhood community stakeholders to assist with the study design, analysis, and interpretation of results. This coalition included staff from the GOECD, the Illinois Head Start Association, the Ounce of Prevention Fund (Start Early), Illinois Action for Children, and faculty from early childhood education training programs, master practitioners, and early childhood program administrators. This coalition met to review initial survey results, identify priority analyses, and review and critique a planned qualitative interview script and analysis plan. A second coalition meeting was held after the preliminary coding of follow-up interviews when a fuller presentation of results yielded different analytical priorities. The coalition also identified key audiences for presentations and assisted with disseminating the final report. A subset of this coalition stayed on to help devise subsequent longitudinal follow-up surveys in 2019 and 2020.

In each year of the study, a link to the online survey was disseminated in the summer inquiring about program practices, policies, and experiences in the prior academic year. To participate, respondents had to serve in an administrative role in an Illinois early childhood program serving children between birth and 5 years of age. Like many studies of expulsion in early childhood, this study used a convenience sampling approach. Members of the coalition and my other networks and partnerships helped spread the word. We sent information out over regional and statewide child-care and early childhood provider listservs, posted in social media groups, put blurbs in network and professional organization newsletters, and e-blasted training program alumni lists. Nearly 500 administrators participated over 4 years, 36 of whom participated each year (our longitudinal repeat sample). Although it is impossible to know how representative this sample was (since there is no full statewide database of providers from all program types), we collected surveys from a wide array of programs. Responses came from center-, home- and school-based providers, representing urban and non-urban communities. Multiple sources often funded programs, including private-pay tuition, child-care assistance vouchers, state and federal public initiative funding, and Head Start. In the first year of the study covering the 2017–2018 school year, we also conducted follow-up interviews with a subsample of 25 administrators (these interviews were also discussed in Chapter 6). We recruited participants for the interviews based on their survey responses. The coalition wanted to be sure they understood, in greater detail, the experiences of administrators who knew a great deal about the law and those who knew relatively little. Additionally, we made sure to balance the sample to represent those in urban and non-urban parts of the state.

In addition to querying about the programs' structure, size, funding, and knowledge of the law, we asked a series of targeted questions about exclusionary discipline rates. Administrators were asked to report how many times in the past 12 months: (1) a parent was asked to pick up their child early from school (early pick-ups), (2) a parent was asked to keep their child at home temporarily (suspensions), or (3) a child was asked to permanently leave the program due to behavioral concerns (expulsions). Beginning in the 2018–2019 survey, we also asked specifically about the number of children transitioning to another program and the number of children withdrawn by parents because the program could not accommodate the child's needs. Full details about this study were published in a 2021 special issue of the American Psychological Association's journal *Translational Issues in Psychological Science* and in brief reports. Below, I provide an overview of key findings and their implications both within Illinois and more broadly. The interpretation of these evaluation findings was a collaborative effort, and I am indebted to my coauthors on that article, especially Allison Lowe-Fotos, Maria Estlund, and Lori Orr.

Evaluating the Implementation of Illinois PA 100-0105

Across the board, results from the study validated initial efforts in crafting the legislation. Rates of expulsion declined over the 3 study years. During the 2017–2018 school year during which the law initially went into effect, nearly half (48%) of programs had sent at least one child home early, and a third each had suspended at least one child (32%) and expelled at least one child (35%). Overall, 12 out of every 1,000 children served across all participating programs were expelled that year due to challenging behaviors. This rate was almost *twice* the national average for state prekindergarten programs reported by Walter Gilliam in 2005. However, one year later, less than 3 out of every 1,000 enrolled children under the age of 5 were permanently expelled, and suspension and early dismissal incidences similarly dropped off. In subsequent years, rates rose slightly (3.4 per 1,000 children enrolled in the 2020–2021 survey), but the closures and disruptions due to COVID-19 make interpreting recent data more complicated. Regardless, the precipitous decline from the original survey is dramatic and provides preliminary evidence of the effectiveness of the legislative effort. Importantly, however, just looking at the formal expulsion rates does not tell the full story.

As mentioned above, starting in the second year of the study, we included questions about planned transitions and voluntary withdrawals (i.e., push-outs or soft expulsions). While rates of formal expulsions dropped significantly in 2018–2019, these other exclusion pathways suggest that programs found or maintained other options for removing challenging children. Specifically, 6.35 of every 1,000 children served were voluntarily withdrawn by their families due to behavioral challenges. Administrators reported that an additional 3 per 1,000 were transitioned out. However, when we examined open-ended responses to questions about this transition process, it became clear that most of these cases would not meet the law's definition of a planned transition. That is, programs often counted handing parents a list of local programs and telling them to call around as "helping to plan the transition." When added together, the formal and soft expulsions plus the reported transitions in 2018–2019 still reached almost the same level of exclusion (11 per 1,000) as in 2017–2018.

In subsequent years, while rates of formal expulsion have remained stable, informal exclusions have increased. In the 2020–2021 survey (administered in the fall of 2021), participating administrators reported planning the transitions for nearly 20 out of every 1,000 enrolled children. Discussions following our recent data presentations to policymakers, advocates, and practitioners indicate collective uncertainty about whether increasing the frequency of planned transitions is a desirable outcome or an unintended consequence. As one mental health consultant quipped to me, "it's just another way to not be inclusive."

When we disaggregate data by program type, we get a more nuanced story about discipline practices—in 2017–2018, exclusionary discipline systematically varied by program characteristics, lending credence to advocate's original adamancy about PA 100-0105 applying to all state-funded or licensed programs. Center-based programs expelled significantly more children than home- or school-based programs, and those receiving public dollars expelled more children than those that only accepted private tuition.

When I presented these results to the Early Childhood Inter-agency Team charged with implementing the legislation across agencies, the policymakers had a robust discussion about the different mechanisms at play. For example, in a mixed-delivery system, variation in funding may be impacting a program's ability or desire to retain a child displaying challenging behaviors. Public funding streams, like the Child Care Assistance Program (CCAP) reimbursements, typically provide less money per child than a program would receive from tuition-paying parents, and it is rarely enough to support best practices in meeting children's social-emotional and behavioral needs. Therefore, children and their families paying tuition may be particularly coveted, increasing a program's likelihood of working with them through challenging behaviors. Pushing out tuition-paying families also likely concerned providers because it could negatively impact their reputations in the community. One provider we interviewed spoke candidly about being afraid of getting a negative review on Google or Yelp because that could ruin her whole business. In a similar vein, even though home-based childcare programs are expelling children less often, interviews indicated that they are often where children end up when they have been expelled from center-based care. Center administrators reported suggesting that families of "challenging" children seek out smaller settings where the child could receive more one-on-one attention. When discussed by the coalition, this theme raised some concerns—not because home-based care settings would not be wonderful caring spaces for these children, but because so much less is known about their capacity, access to resources such as consultation, and support for reflection and development. These programs also tend to be the last to receive new information and may be more precariously funded. While efforts are made to decrease the exclusion rates overall, advocates agreed that there was an immediate need for resources and information to be funneled to home-based programs to support the needs of previously excluded children and the adults who care for them. This study's findings pushed members of the coalition to think critically about how funding mechanisms are associated with both positive and unintended outcomes for children and families.

Beginning with the 2018–2019 survey, administrators reported on the demographic characteristics of the excluded children, and despite the declining rates in overall exclusion, familiar patterns of inequity have doggedly remained. In 2018–2019, while just over half of children enrolled in participating programs were boys, they made up 86% of children excluded. At the same time, girls were slightly over-represented among those voluntarily withdrawn by their parents. Black children were similarly over-represented across all types of exclusion, but especially among those formally expelled. In the 2019–2020 survey, while less than 17% of enrolled students identified as Black or African American, they made up 33% of those formally expelled. By comparison, when White children were excluded, they were more likely to be voluntarily withdrawn. Older children (4- and 5-year-olds) tended to be over-represented across all types of exclusion as well.

Like the findings regarding children's early adverse experiences reported in Chapter 3 (Zeng et al., 2019), we saw high levels of ACEs in this sample. Half of the excluded children we have data on from 2018–2019 had unemployed or divorced parents. A third of excluded children experienced food insecurity, and more than a quarter had insecure housing situations. 40% each had witnessed or been the victim of violence, and nearly a quarter had a parent who was incarcerated.

As we have seen with K–12 expulsion policy changes (Losen et al., 2015), reductions in overall exclusion rates have not eliminated gender and racial disparities. Even accounting for limitations in the child-level data, children who were older, Black, or boys were over-represented among those excluded. These findings suggest that superficial nods toward equity, such as referencing racial and gender disparities and implicit bias training in the legislation, will likely be ineffective. The results regarding children's exposures to adversity further emphasize the need for robust social-emotional supports in all program types and the pressure teachers are placed under to master trauma-informed care principles. Accountability and data systems to track overall rates of exclusion and proportionality of disciplinary procedures will be critical to ensure disciplinary equity.

Another key priority of the coalitions was to identify gaps in disseminating information about the law and persistent areas of confusion. Given the fractured oversight of early care and education across the state, stakeholders were unsure whether information about the new law was well disseminated to all types of programs. On average, administrators indicated they felt moderately knowledgeable about the law, but this rating showed significant variance. Those working in programs receiving some public funding, especially those at school-based or Head Start programs, were much more likely to identify themselves as knowledgeable. Home-based providers were least likely to report feeling well-informed.

As a parent, Aiden's mother, Lydia, should not have known more about child-care regulations than her son's teachers and the program director. And yet, information about the Illinois expulsion law was slow to make its way into the professional networks, especially for private independent programs. Our analysis of the 2017–2018 data found that administrators who had recently expelled at least one child were significantly more knowledgeable about the law than those with no expulsion history, indicating that many programs likely learned by doing. Interactions with well-informed parents or social service agencies like Easter Seals, during or after an expulsion, seemed to be among the most potent means of disseminating information about the law.

In the interviews, we more objectively assessed specific knowledge in the interviews by asking administrators to recall precise details about the law. While the vast majority could remember the central tenet that expulsions were now prohibited, a third also reported inaccurate information about the law, such as that it only applied to preschool-age children, children with diagnosed disabilities, or those funded through CCAP vouchers. These misunderstandings persisted. In the following year (2018–2019), we asked administrators to respond to a series of scenarios about children leaving care and found that many still believed the law only applied to specific age-bands, while others thought that the law did not apply to home-based care.

These misinterpretations would have clear consequences for families. There was also a great deal of confusion about the planned transition stipulation. Over 60% of administrators completing the second survey in 2018–2019 thought that simply providing a family with a list of local programs constituted a planned transition. Further, nearly half of administrators thought that keeping a child in the director's office for multiple days until the family could find alternative care was sufficient to comply with the law's requirement that they "exhaust all resources and supports."

These data were collected in the period between when the law was passed and the DCFS and ISBE rules were published, which may have contributed to the confusion. Advocates had hoped that the rules would better define and lay out procedures for these transitions. Based on my review of the public comments to the initial rule drafts, however, it is clear that many stakeholders remain doubtful. Early childhood administrators in Illinois have previously reported being overwhelmed with licensing requirements and supervisory tasks (Main et al., 2018) and do not have a means by which to necessarily identify and arrange suitable alternative programming. Further, as we saw in Chapter 5 with Jace and Ms. Elena, even when an administrator has deep community connections and can work the phones to find an alternate program, these transitions can easily fall through. Findings from this ongoing evaluation suggest a need for a regional match-making service that can help families and administrators identify the needs of a child and locate programs with immediate openings that fit a family's unique needs.

Coalition members used the findings of administrators' confusion and inaccurate knowledge about the law to facilitate broader dissemination of information about the legislation and to bolster recommendations to state agencies as rules were being drafted and available for public comment. In response to the widespread lack of knowledge and confusion about how to comply with PA 100-0105 captured by this study, public awareness presentations and a Training of Trainers series was created. Statewide, 188 professional development providers attended a workshop on the legislation and related best practice recommendations. Findings from this study informed how the workshop leaders presented information to participants, and leaders reported that when results were included in the training, practitioners felt that their experiences and frustrations were validated.

Findings from this study also shed light on some of the barriers that programs experienced accessing the prevention resources outlined in the legislation, especially infant and early childhood mental health consultation. Despite consultation services being free to all child-care programs, less than half of respondents had ever worked with a consultant in the first year. Of those that had, a quarter of interviewed administrators reported excessive wait times, sometimes up to several months. The law explicitly cites consultation as a resource that should be used to prevent expulsion, and these findings highlighted the fact that there is a statewide need to expand the pool of consultants. The scarcity resulted both in programs forming negative impressions of the intervention, and in consultation being misused as a crisis intervention rather than the long-term, proactive/preventive, relationship-based support it is designed to serve as (see Chapter 8).

This finding directly informed the state's prioritization of infrastructure and professional development in their application for funding through the federal Preschool Development Grant Birth to Five (PDG B-5). In outlining how they would use the renewal awarded to Illinois in November 2019, the GOECD put children's mental health in the forefront by proposing to develop a statewide database of consultants and better regional supports and supervision to enhance practice (among other initiatives). Additionally, when results were presented to the state's Children's Mental Health Partnership leadership team meeting in 2019, the findings spurred discussion of consolidating infant and early childhood mental health consultation under a shared service delivery model to ensure equity in access.

Across the country, states and municipalities are working to address the nation's early childhood discipline crisis. Each approach must be tailored to the local context and work around or through existing structures and regulations. However, we must ensure that these policy efforts have broad and equitable impacts, in addition to being nuanced. Although our context is unique, the case study of Illinois provides a concrete example of one path forward. The path was not smooth by any means. Advocates and stakeholders spent years crafting and passing the law, and it still has not been fully implemented as was intended. Just as Illinois's advocates gained technical assistance and encouragement from other states and national advocates (e.g., the BUILD initiative), hopefully the results of this evaluation study can help other jurisdictions avoid some pitfalls. At the same time, our findings paint a complex picture. The Illinois expulsion law was not a panacea, and exclusionary discipline is still being used and in ways that unfairly target boys and Black children. Sometimes, being in a trailblazing state means that lessons are learned through mistakes and missteps. But without mechanisms to capture providers' voice on the frontline, instances of misunderstanding, anxiety, and avoidance would go undetected.

Our research-practice-policy coalition was critical not only to the successful collection of these evaluation data, but also to the immediate translation of findings into tangible changes in improved services and enhanced funding. This coalition facilitates a feedback loop that continues to reap benefits for the state's legislation and rule-making process while validating providers' experiences. Just as in early education classrooms, our collective learning continues to depend on relationships grounded in mutual trust and commitment to improving the lives of young children in Illinois and the professionals who care for them. As a researcher, my students and I had to be good listeners and adjust our methods and aims to meet the stakeholders' needs. Likewise, state agencies had to make themselves vulnerable to challenging results and engage in reflective policymaking. As the number of laws around exclusionary discipline in early childhood across the country has continued to increase over recent years (Davis et al., 2020; Meek et al., 2020), research on its implementation and impact must keep up.

10
Conclusion

Like thousands of other children across the country in 2020, Lance started first grade at his kitchen table with hybrid remote instruction. "It's been rough . . . but he's doing well," Stephen reported when we touched base late that year. "As much as we try, it's impossible to give him the same education and resources that school can, like personalized teaching, speech therapy, a social worker. . . . It's hard to replace that at home."

While learning from home is a new challenge for the whole family, working without full-time child care is all too familiar. Stephen missed countless hours of work while Lance was repeatedly expelled and excluded from preschool. By Stephen's report, Lance is still feeling the lingering effects of those exclusions too. "The experiences still hurt him today. He remembers so much, and he struggles with impulsive behavior and rejections. We drive by old daycares, and he still says, 'I got kicked out of that school.' It's so sad. Even now, more than two years later, he brings up experiences where he was isolated and kept alone."

Lance recalls specific events and talks regularly about his negative experiences in the child-care programs that rejected him. Stephen also worries about what Lance is not telling them and what he does not remember. "We were so hurt and saddened that Lance went through all this. There is no telling what he endured that he can't tell us. People need to know Lance's story. Some of these horrible experiences still haunt this little boy today, and the damage may last for years or life."

* * *

The children behind the statistics in Walter Gilliam's seminal report on early childhood expulsions are in their 20s now, and there is no way to identify them and know the impact of the expulsions on them and their families. Unfortunately, the same is true of children being expelled today. Despite attention from the national media, policymakers, and researchers, we have no longitudinal data on the effect of early exclusion specifically. We also do not yet know enough to prevent stories like Lance's. As much as the preceding chapters in this book shed light on the numerous and complex correlates of expulsion, my writing does not provide a satisfying answer to Stephen's questions: How do we stop it from happening? What will be the lingering effects for the thousands of expelled, excluded, and pushed-out kids? My intention, however, is that by amassing what we do know in this text, we can continue to keep the conversation alive. Expulsions did not magically fade away with the passage of a few new policies. It will take continued collective action and more substantial research to understand how to effectively end the practice for good.

When a child's first experience with schooling is one of rejection, it is bound to leave a stain. However, even though expulsion rates in early childhood are triple that of school-age populations, we still know comparatively little about the practice's causes and consequences. In a recent systematic review of studies of exclusionary discipline in K–12 settings, Richard Welsh and Shafiqua Little (2018) analyzed over 180 studies meeting their inclusion criteria. When my research team followed parallel search procedures in the early childhood literature in the fall of 2020, we found only 20 published studies that included measures of suspension or expulsion (Zinsser et al., 2022). Methodologically, the early childhood expulsion literature base has a long way to go, too. Most studies we reviewed used correlational analyses and cross-sectional designs, which prevents us from making any causal inferences. Researchers also often relied on convenience samples, making it challenging to generalize findings to larger populations. As we saw in my evaluation of the Illinois legislation, these convenience samples are also at times unwilling to provide complete demographic data, making inferences impossible. Without a sufficient and rigorous evidence base, policymakers are left to legislate in the dark, and practitioners and families are left inadequately supported.

There are also critical gaps in our knowledge at every level of the ecological model. Only a handful of published early childhood studies included child-level data about those expelled. Very few published studies assessed structural factors such as teacher education or years of experience. There was also limited attention to administrative practices or policies. Thankfully the research base is steadily growing. More than half of the studies in our systematic review were published between 2017 and 2020 and covered various settings serving diverse populations.

Looking across this literature base, it is clear that exclusion likely cannot be wholly prevented through simple policy mandates like requiring educators to complete more years of education or training. Instead, research has continually homed in on the intra-personal factors touched on in Chapter 5. Nearly half of the studies to date assessed factors such as teacher well-being (e.g., stress and depression), workplace experiences (e.g., efficacy and use of available resources), and perceptions (e.g., of parents and accountability). When combined with what is known about practitioners' high rates of trauma and inadequate compensation, this review's findings highlight the fact that efforts to reduce exclusion must include adequate and multifaceted support for the well-being of these educators. Unfortunately, across the interventions and policies developed to prevent expulsion, workplace factors have not been meaningfully addressed. According to the scan of state policies discussed in the preceding chapter (McCann, Smith, Nguyen, & Granja, 2021), there is little to no effort to use policy to meaningfully alter early childhood educators' working conditions as a way to prevent expulsions. For example, only four states encourage programs to revise staffing patterns to ensure reasonable working hours and breaks. Only one state recommends that programs increase paid planning time for staff. Two each mention decreasing ratios or group sizes.

Instead of addressing expulsion by improving working conditions, states seem to be expecting more of teachers. The majority of states indicated that teachers should broadly increase their knowledge and skills (e.g., in developmentally appropriate practice, family engagement, using SEL curriculum, and culturally and linguistically responsive care) without necessarily providing the time, finances, or other resources to do so. While we as a nation decry the practice of expulsion, through our policy, it is clear that we place all of the blame and the responsibility for reform on the backs of teachers whom we have collectively ignored, undervalued, and disempowered for decades.

Two members of the Children's Equity Project, Shantel Meek and Evandra Catherine, concluded their powerful November 2020 *Washington Post* article by quoting Maya Angelou, writing, "Do the best you can until you know better. Then, when you know better, do better." We've known about the early childhood expulsion crisis for quite a while, and on the surface, it appears that we are doing better. The trend we saw in the Illinois evaluation study is happening across the country. New data released from the Office of Civil Rights in the U.S. Department of Education shows that between the 2015–2016 and 2017–2018 school years, rates of public preschool expulsion were coming down. The national attention to early childhood exclusion, investment in children's mental health and teacher training, and guidance for policy efforts seem to be working on the surface. Unfortunately, as Meek and Catherine lament, "all of that action still wasn't enough" to disrupt the persistent disparities. Black boys are still over-represented in the Office of Civil Rights' most recent reporting, and Black girls are even more starkly over-represented than before. Black girls make up 19% of all female enrollment but are 53% of all girls excluded. When policies explicitly cite disproportionate discipline as a motivator for their passage but do not adequately fund and implement genuine anti-racist reforms, it is not surprising that those who were the impetus are still left out as rates recede. We've seen similar trends in K–12 schooling, where average rates of expulsions and suspensions decrease, but disparities persist.

Why disciplinary disparities exist in early childhood also remains an open question. As we reviewed in Chapter 4, research in school-age children has pointed to the potential contributions of uneven or biased disciplinary policies, discriminatory practices, and under-resourced or inadequate support for teachers. Descriptive reports from state and local agencies have replicated the disparities in early childhood settings. But descriptive analyses add little to our understanding of processes and associated factors predicting exclusion. To determine whether exclusion pathways differ across vulnerable subgroups, researchers will need to conduct inferential analyses with robust data that allow for disaggregation. From a strengths-based perspective, we would also do well to think about how to identify and validate teaching practices that challenge inequity and prevent disproportionate discipline. New observational measurement techniques like the Assessing Classroom Sociocultural Equity Scale developed by Drs. Stephanie Curenton and colleagues (Curenton et al., 2020) can help us codify and celebrate inclusive classroom practices. At present, however, such practices are not included in definitions of quality held up by state licensing and accrediting bodies.

Throughout this text, I have repeated the call for more and better data. This may sound like desperate pleading by an analytically crazed academic, but without accurate, holistic data from all early care and education system sectors, we cannot truly understand the problem's scope. Without data that can be disaggregated by race, gender, and disability status, we cannot know whether the interventions and policies being implemented benefit all children or only a privileged few. The adage *what is measured is treasured* works in reverse as well. We, as a society, do not value our youngest learners, nor those who care for them. This neglect is evident in how we reimburse programs for only a small fraction of the real cost of high-quality care. It is evident in the abysmal compensation and lack of professional respect given to educators.

We even discount the hard intellectual work of toddlers and preschoolers learning critical skills to navigate our society. Worse yet, for generations, we have chronically underfunded the systems of care available to marginalized communities of color, despite the fact that we have evidenced the impact of early education in these populations (e.g., the Perry Preschool project cited in the opening chapter of this book).

Children of color and those from indigenous or migrant families have been routinely relegated to lower-quality programs that lack sufficient resources and critical support access. As a result of our persistent under-investment in our nation's ad hoc "system" of early care and education, we have collectively built a flawed structure for assessing the impact of our investments. If we genuinely wish to dismantle the school-to-prison pipeline, to prevent the costly and harmful effects of exclusion, we have to start where the pipeline begins—in early care and education. Unfortunately, without better mechanisms for collecting, disaggregating, and analyzing data before children's school entry, policymakers, advocates, parents, and practitioners are left in the dark.

The expulsion of any young child is an unfortunate reminder of our inadequate early childhood system. That most of the children being pushed out are Black and Brown, despite bans and guidelines against the practice, is a reminder of the persistent smog of racism in our early childhood classrooms. By no means am I the first to make this plea, and mine will not be the most definitive voice. It will take a chorus of all of us, a loud and exasperated chorus calling for proper investment in our youngest learners and their caregivers and teachers. We have no time left to lose.

Creating a Healing Village: An Afterword

Iheoma U. Iruka, Ph.D.

It is about 9:30 a.m. and a frigid day in the Midwest. I am in what is considered a high-quality lab school, and I am doing a tour to get a sense of how a particular curriculum works in this classroom. I can observe the classroom through an observation deck, which is equipped with a video and microphone. I am in this observation deck with three other colleagues. What I witness is not something unusual, but something that hurts and angers me. I see him, a 4-year-old Black boy named Jonathan [pseudonym], looking up now and then at one of his teachers close by as he builds what seems to be a complex track system for his train. This teacher, Ms. Narac [pseudonym], is engaged in conversation with two other children who look White. As she gets up, Jonathan looks up to see if she will notice his complex track system. She does not. Ms. Narac steps over this track system, never making eye contact with him, as she walks from one side of the classroom to another side of the classroom and begins to engage in a back-and-forth conversation with another White student. Jonathan continues to build his track, and a few of his friends join him in his track-making, and gets even more excited and vocal, only to be told by Ms. Narac, "please keep it down, Jonathan." Jonathan keeps it down for a few seconds only to get a bit more animated. Then Ms. Narac walks over, seemingly angry or agitated, looks down at him, and says to him, "it is time to put away your materials, Jonathan, and move to the reading circle." She never talks about how quietly he worked for over 15 minutes, the joy he and his peers were having due to his activity, the complexity of his work, and why he was getting animated. Unfortunately, this interaction is consistent with Jonathan's experience at this "high-quality lab school."

* * *

Exclusionary practices are not always loud, violent, and angry words. Exclusionary practice can also include subtle interactions like microinvalidations and microaggressions that remind children about their powerlessness, their faults, and that evoke sensitive feelings of not belonging or being less than. These exclusionary practices and interactions are also harmful and traumatic for the child and other children in the program. These interactions may set the framework for how children believe they may be treated by adults, so they become hypervigilant to these exclusionary experiences. National early childhood studies note that teachers report having less close and more conflictual relationships with their Black students (Jerome et al., 2009).

Science is clear about the importance of the first few years of life. The early years are crucial for setting the foundation for brain development in language, vision, hearing, conceptualization, numbers, emotion control, and memory. There is some consensus about what matters and what impacts children's early development (Shonkoff, Phillips, & National Research Council, 2000; National Academies of Sciences, Engineering, and Medicine [NASEM], 2019). These consensuses include: (a) biology and environment shape development, which work in tandem and have lifelong consequences; (b) adult-child attachments are building blocks for children's outcomes; (c) children's trajectories are vulnerable to adversities, including experiences across contexts from home to early care and education settings; (d) adversities, such as poverty, racism, discrimination, and other exclusionary actions, may disrupt optimal development for children; and (e) the early years are when interventions and protective factors are most effective and can potentially disrupt the impacts of adversities on children. For Jonathan and his family, this early care and education program is supposed to serve as his vital village that provides protection and affirmation from psychological harm and feelings of exclusion.

Studies indicate that Jonathan's relationship with Ms. Narac is setting a precedent for future relationships as he matriculates through school (Hamre & Pianta, 2001; Iruka et al., 2010; Jerome et al., 2009). In a National Bureau of Economic Research working paper by Gershenson and colleagues (2018), they found that Black students who'd had just one Black teacher by third grade were 13 percent more likely to enroll in college—and those who'd had two were 32 percent more likely. The authors postulated that these findings are because of "role model effects" with Black teachers affirming and confirming for Black students that education matters. Thus, teachers are in a powerful position to set a tone and expectations—good or bad—for what children should expect in their relationship with teachers and their learning environment.

Our seminal early care and education interventions, such as the HighScope Perry Preschool Program and the Carolina Abecedarian Study, as well as the first pilots of Head Start, primarily involved Black children and their families. These interventions provide insight into the importance of early care and education on children's cognitive and language development and socio-emotional development that are critical drivers to supporting children's school and life success. Unfortunately, Black children compared to other children are less likely to be in high-quality early learning settings (Barnett et al., 2013), at least based on current metrics of quality, even though they are more likely to be in non-parental child-care arrangements in the first year of life (Cui & Natzke, 2020). This is probably because Black parents, especially Black mothers, have always been in the labor force and are likely to work retail and hourly wage jobs that don't offer paid family medical leave or sick benefits or other job securities (Gould & Wilson, 2020). Simultaneously, Black children are also likely to live in poverty (Creamer, 2020; Thomas & Fry, 2020), to experience adverse childhood experiences (Morsy & Rothstein, 2019), and to live in concentrated disadvantage (Jargowsky, 2015). Even when they receive early care and education access, they are more likely to be suspended or expelled (Office for Civil Rights, 2016). This is what one would call a "trifecta of insults:" (1) Black children are likely to come from poor households or to live in concentrated disadvantage; (2) Black children were the primary participants in studies that substantiated the importance of early childhood education for school and life outcomes; and (3) when they get access, Black children are likely to not get the full dosage due to suspension, expulsion, or exclusionary practices and policies. Whether subtle (as in Jonathan's case) or egregious, these exclusionary practices send a message for Black children to feel that they will never be seen as belonging and will never be protected from the psychological trauma occurring outside and inside the walls of the schools or programs. This is likely the reason we have the preschool-to-prison pipeline, rather than what should be our focus, the cradle-to-career pipeline (Adamu & Hogan, 2015).

Expulsions and suspensions are a symptom of a larger problem that has often dehumanized and suppressed the excellence and joy in learning for Black children. It is one that is focused on exclusionary policies and practices, such as over-identification of children in special education categories like emotionally disturbed and learning disabled, and under-identification in autism, low expectations, and limited access to enriching, child-driven, and rigorous curricula (Ford & Russo, 2016; Morgan et al., 2017). This is a system that, while it makes a note of the value of centering the classroom environment and learning based on children's context, learning style, and interest, is still a system replete and hyper-focused on pathologizing certain groups of children (i.e., Black, Indigenous). The treatment of young Black children is a microcosm of how the United States views Black people—as pathological "sub-humans" who need to be controlled and not afforded freedom of self, and when they seem uncontrollable, must be subdued. This is why preschool teachers implicitly monitor (i.e., hypervigilance) Black children, especially Black boys, for a potential sign of a problem and one they must intervene in to protect the other children (i.e., White children) (Gilliam et al., 2016).

In her 2005 paper, Yosso highlights the strengths and assets of Black communities, including:

- aspirational capital (maintain hopes and dreams for the future regardless of barriers);
- linguistic capital (intellectual and social skills attained through communication experiences in more than one language, style, or dialect);
- familial capital (cultural knowledge nurtured among kin that carries a sense of community history, memory, and cultural intuition;
- social capital (networks of people and community resources that provide support to navigate through society's institutions); and
- navigational capital (skills of maneuvering through social institutions not created for communities of color), to name a few.

Unfortunately, these aspects of cultural wealth are not part of the curriculum, standards, family programming, measures, or even early care and education assessments. Much of the early childhood community is primarily focused on the poor outcomes of Black children and families, often neglecting the historical legacy of anti-Black racism and its continued manifestation in all aspects of children's and their families' daily experience. It is time that we shift from a focus on just negatives and deficits to one that truly sees our complicity in ignoring our role in the poor outcomes and the invisibility of the cultural strengths and wealth of Black communities. How can Jonathan's teacher see his strength in the classroom, instead of being hyper-focused on his exuberance as negative rather than as an expression of the joy of learning?

This book is a reminder of the TED Talk "The Danger of a Single Story" by Chimamanda Ngozi Adichie, which warned about the peril of hearing only one story about a person, a country, or even a situation, resulting in grave misunderstandings and ineffective resolutions. To find an effective solution to a major problem like preschool suspension, expulsion, and exclusionary practices, we must look at all of the root causes and the reverberations of particular practices and policies on the entire community. We must also reflect on the reverberations of what we see as potential solutions. While we recognize the impact of exclusionary practices on children and their families, there is also an effect on other children, educators, and the larger early childhood community.

In this book, Katherine Zinsser leads readers on a journey that humanizes and crystallizes the complexity of suspensions and expulsions in early care and education. She bursts the myth of Black children being the reason for their disproportionate expulsion, suspension, and exclusion, which is often couched as a "child problem" due to historical and intergenerational racism and trauma, rather than adult behaviors in decision-making. She also reminds readers that early educators, on average, are stressed, depressed, unheard, underpaid, and undervalued, and this combination has an impact on micro and macro interactions between educators and children in their classroom. How do we protect and affirm children and early educators, especially for early educators who are highly stressed, depressed, underpaid, and undervalued, working in low-resourced early education settings?

The National Association for the Education of Young Children (NAEYC) reminds us that it is a moral, ethical, and professional obligation to provide safe, healthy, affirming, and enriching learning environments and to engage with children in a way that honors their self-identity and brings out their best. Thus, it is up to adults, including parents, early educators, and community members, to provide protection, affection, redirection (formerly correction), and connection for children, especially Black children who often experience racial trauma (Anderson et al., 2019; Winn et al., 2012). *Protection* is the intentional sheltering from, instruction about, and monitoring of threats or harm to a person's physical, emotional, and cultural identities. Children deserve physically and emotionally safe spaces free from violence and ridicule, low educational expectations, and shaming, where compassion is the norm, and children's behaviors are viewed as assets and not deficits. *Affection* is the intentional affirmation, caring, and nurturance of a person's physical, social, emotional, and cultural identity. The purpose of affection is the affirmation that children are valued and important. Showing affection means that adults provide healthy, predictable, consistent nurturance and support as children try new behaviors, learn new constructs, and try, fail, and succeed at mastering new material or environments. *Redirection*, formerly called correction, is the intentional support for healthy, adaptive behaviors while confronting maladaptive behaviors that undermine children's physical, emotional, cultural identity, humanity, and voice. The purpose of redirection is not punishment but accountability, reconciliation, and the building, enhancing, or reconnecting of children to their best selves, families, and others. *Connection* is about social, emotional, and cultural connections. The purpose of connection is to foster a sense of belonging, value, purpose, uniqueness, and being necessary to the larger community's (or education environment's) success. These protective ingredients—protection, affection, redirection, and connection—should be used as the focal driver for decision-making to truly meet the needs of children and the educators who care for and teach them. The conversation about exclusionary policies must focus on creating healing spaces through practices and policies that focus on protection, affection, redirection, and connection of our young children.

> *I have never encountered any children in any group who are not geniuses. There is no mystery on how to teach them. The first thing you do is treat them like human beings and the second thing you do is love them.*
>
> —Dr. Asa Hilliard

Acknowledgments

I would not recommend trying to write your first book during a global pandemic. Certainly not one on the value and necessity of early learning during the ironic closure of your children's preschool. While I did gain some needed perspective and an extra dose of empathy for child-care workers, this experience has mostly filled me with gratitude. Despite the social reckoning and calamity around us, many people went out of their way to help bring this book to life.

First and foremost, I want to thank the parents of children who have been excluded—both those who spoke with me for this book and anyone who has been through the ordeal. Thank you for speaking up, for sharing your stories, and for helping to try to prevent it from happening to anyone else. You and your children deserve to be loved and cherished. My only hope is that this text can shine a light into these dark places in our fragile system.

I am also incredibly grateful to the hundreds of early childhood professionals whom I have interviewed, surveyed, and worked with in trying to understand why and how children come to be excluded. From the teachers talking vulnerably about their fear and frustration in the classroom to the administrators who feel trapped by funding and regulatory systems, I earnestly appreciate your openness and honesty in speaking with me. I want to thank the practitioners who inspired and informed this book. Special thanks go to Kim Kull, Lesley Kruter, and Katie Conklin, who welcomed me into their centers and made tangible the constraints and joys of directing early learning programs.

The actual writing of this book was made possible by two groups of early educators. First, I am indebted to the teachers and staff at La Casa Montessori in Oak Park, Illinois, who have kept my whole family safe, happy, and loved both in-person and virtually during a tumultuous year. Likewise, I want to acknowledge Hope Prosky and the teachers of Grace Church Nursery School in Brooklyn, New York, who nurtured my love of learning and compassion many years ago.

The production of this book relied on the work of hundreds of talented researchers, trailblazers, and mentors for whom I am grateful. Chief among these is my doctoral advisor, Susanne Denham, who helped me find my way from juvenile justice research to circle time on the carpet, where I first understood the power and grace of early childhood education. Tim Curby is one of the only reasons I kept writing during the depths of quarantine. Nearly a dozen years into our joint research endeavors, you are still a bright light and an inspiration. Thank you for being flexible, generous with time and authorship, and a great friend. Special thanks to my colleagues at the University of Illinois at Chicago who have inspired, encouraged, and checked in on me: Bette Bottoms, who helped me find a home for this book, and Amanda Roy, Jess Shaw, and Sarai Coba-Rodriguez, who have kept me grounded in a social justice mission. Cathy Main, without your guidance and mentorship these past 8 years, I would never have found my footing in Illinois early childhood. Thank you for being my glossary, way-finder, and champion at the state and city levels. While writing this book, I also said goodbye to a dear colleague, Roger Weissberg. Roger was the reason I came to UIC and motivated me to leave the safe simplicity of the academy and embrace the community stance of this work. His passion to change systems to benefit children and families was infectious and I strive to pay it forward every day.

I would be remiss not to thank my current and former students who inspired, cheered, and tolerated me. Courtney Zulauf-McCurdy, Callie Silver, Luz Torres, and Christen Park—you all have been tremendous thought partners, and I am grateful to have had a chance to learn alongside you. A special thanks, also, to my former student, turned lab manager, turned friend, Tito Ponce. You took the reins and kept us all moving forward even during the darkest days of 2020. Kay Thursby, thank you for helping get this over the finish line and providing excellent support in the final phases.

I am eternally grateful that the National Academy of Education and the Spencer Foundation took a risk on me and funded my first study of expulsion in 2015. Through that postdoctoral fellowship, I was connected with mentors such as Hiro Yoshikawa of New York University (who was the first to tell me to write a book) and Paul Morgan of Pennsylvania State University. My collaborative work focusing on Illinois state policy has also been funded by the American Psychological Association's Division 207 (Society for Community Research & Action), the Robert Wood Johnson Foundation, and the Office of Social Science Research at the University of Illinois at Chicago, and the Society for the Psychological Study of Social Issues. Writing retreats and coaching with the Institute for Research on Race and Public Policy at UIC and Jill Petty were a reliable source of inspiration, community, and clarity.

To my colleagues on the Illinois Association for Infant Mental Health board, thank you for helping me appreciate the multitude of challenges facing children and providers across the state. Thanks also for connecting me with deeply insightful consultants who opened up about their work and experiences. Norma Irie, Anne Konen, and Rosa Ortiz of Illinois Action for Children and Annie Davis of the Center of Excellence, thank you for helping me understand the nuances of this powerful intervention.

To my guides and thought partners in Illinois early childhood policy—Allison Lowe-Fotos, Lorri Orr, and Maria Estlund—thank you for your patience with me and willingness to answer questions, go down rabbit holes, and promote our collective work.

Ann and Tony Zinsser—Mom and Dad—thank you for your decades of unconditional support and encouragement. I know how lucky I am to have acquired your empathy, curiosity, and persistence. This book sits on the strong foundation you built for me and the opportunities and challenges you surrounded me with.

And finally, my deepest gratitude is for my wife, Caitlin. Any moment I got to write—especially during our first quarantine in the spring of 2020—was made possible by your proactive planning of activities and distractions for our children. We jumped through so many hoops to keep our heads above water during this tumultuous year. You read every page of this book and nearly every page I have written since starting graduate school. I am a writer because of you.

—Katherine Zinsser

References

Adamu, M., & Hogan, L. (2015, October 8). Point of entry: The preschool-to-prison pipeline. *Center for American Progress*. Available from https://www.americanprogress.org/article/point-of-entry/

American Academy of Pediatrics, (2013). Policy statement: Out-of-school suspension and expulsion. *Pediatrics: Official Journal of the American Academy of Pediatrics, 131*, e1000–e1007.

American Psychological Association. (2008). Zero Tolerance Task Force. Are zero tolerance policies effective in the schools? An evidentiary review and recommendations. *American Psychologist, 63*(9), 852–862.

Anderson, R. E., McKenny, M. C., & Stevenson, H. C. (2019). EMBRace: Developing a racial socialization intervention to reduce racial stress and enhance racial coping among black parents and adolescents. *Family Process, 58*(1), 53–67.

Arbeau, K. A., & Coplan, R. J. (2007). Kindergarten teachers' beliefs and responses to hypothetical prosocial, asocial, and antisocial children. *Merrill-Palmer Quarterly, 53*(2), 291–318.

Archambault, I., Janosz, M., Fallu, J. S., & Pagani, L. S. (2009). Student engagement and its relationship with early high school dropout. *Journal of Adolescence, 32*(3), 651–670. https://doi.org/10.1016/j.adolescence.2008.06.007.

Arcia, E. (2006). Achievement and enrollment status of suspended students: Outcomes in a large, multicultural school district. *Education and Urban Society, 38*(3), 359–369. https://doi.org/10.1177/0013124506286947.

Auwarter, A. E., & Aruguete, M. S. (2008). Effects of student gender and socioeconomic status on teacher perceptions. *The Journal of Educational Research, 101*(4), 242–246.

Barnett, S., Carolan, M., & Johns, D. (2013). *Equity and excellence: African-American children's access to quality preschool.* Center on Enhancing Early Learning Outcomes National Institute for Early Education Research Rutgers University. https://nieer.org/wp-content/uploads/2016/08/Equity20and20Excellence20African-American20ChildrenE28099s20Access20to20Quality20Preschool_0.pdf

Bee, D. N. (2012). *An exploratory study of child care center directors' response to young children's challenging behaviors and the impact on preschool expulsion.* Florida State University, Tallahassee, FL. Retrieved from http://purl.flvc.org/fsu/fd/FSU_migr_etd-5320

Bigler, R., Hayes, A. R., & Hamilton, V. (2013). The role of schools in the early socialization of gender differences. In Boivin, Peters, & Tremblay (Eds.), *Encyclopedia on early childhood development* (pp. 1–4). University of Montreal, Canada.

Borg, M. G. (1990). Occupational stress in British educational settings: A review. *Educational Psychology, 10*(2), 103–126.

Bouchard, C., Coutu, S., Bigras, N., Lemay, L., Cantin, G., Bouchard, M. C., & Duval, S. (2015). Perceived, expressed and observed prosociality among four-year-old girls and boys in childcare centres. *Early Child Development and Care, 185*(1), 44–65.

Bradshaw, C. P., Mitchell, M. M., & Leaf, P. J. (2010). Examining the effects of school-wide positive behavioral interventions and supports on student outcomes. *Journal of Positive Behavior Interventions, 12*, 133–148.

Bronfenbrenner, U., & Morris, P. A. (2006). *The bioecological model of human development* (R. M. Lerner, Ed.; 6th ed.). Wiley.

Brotherson, M. J., Summers, J. A., Bruns, D. A., Sharp, L. A. (2008). *Family-centered practices: Working in partnership with families* (P. J. Winton, J. A. McCollum, & C. Catlett, Eds.). Practical.

Buck, K. A., & Ambrosino, R. J. (2004). Children with severe behavior problems: A survey of Texas child care centers' responses. *Early Childhood Education Journal, 31*(4), 241–246.

Campbell, F. A., Ramey, C. T., Pungello, E., Sparling, J., & Miller-Johnson, S. (2002). Early childhood education: Young adult outcomes from the Abecedarian Project. *Applied Developmental Science, 6*(1), 42–57.

Carlson, J. S., Mackrain, M., Van Egeren, L. A., Brophy-Herb, H., Kirk, R., Marciniak, D., Falvay, S., Zheng, Y., Bender, S., & Tableman, B. (2012). Implementing a statewide early childhood mental health consultation approach to preventing childcare expulsion. *Infant Mental Health Journal, 33*(3), 265–273.

Children's Equity Project. (2020). *Start with equity: From the early years to the early grades: Data, research, and actionable child equity policy agenda.* Arizona State University Center for Child and Family Success. https://childandfamilysuccess.asu.edu/cep/start-with-equity

Christle, C. A., Jolivette, K., & Nelson, C. M. (2007). School characteristics related to high school dropout rates. *Remedial and Special Education, 28*, 325–339.

Churchill, S. L. (2003). Goodness-of-fit in early childhood settings. *Early Childhood Education Journal, 31*(2), 113–118.

Clark, K. B., & Clark, M. K. (1939). The development of consciousness of self and the emergence of racial identification in Negro preschool children. *The Journal of Social Psychology, 10*(4), 591–599.

Clayback, K. A., & Hemmeter, M. L. (2021). Exclusionary discipline practices in early childhood settings: A survey of child care directors. *Early Childhood Research Quarterly, 55*, 129–136.

Coba-Rodriguez, S., Cambray-Engstrom, E., & Jarrett, R. L. (2020). The home-based involvement experiences of low-income Latino families with preschoolers transitioning to kindergarten: Qualitative findings. *Journal of Child and Family Studies, 29*(10), 2678–2696.

Condry, J., & Ross, D. (1985). Sex and aggression: The influence of gender label on the perception of aggression in children. *Child Development, 56*(1), 225–233.

Conners Edge, N. A., Kyzer, A., Abney, A., Freshwater, A., Sutton, M., & Whitman, K. (2020). Evaluation of a statewide initiative to reduce expulsion of young children. *Infant Mental Health Journal, 42*(1), 124–139. https://doi.org/10.1002/imhj.21894

Conners Edge, N. A., Rose, A., Honeycutt, D., McKelvey, L., Swindle, T., Courson, D., & Forsman, J. A. (2018). Implementation of Arkansas's initiative to reduce suspension and expulsion of young children. *Journal of Early Intervention, 40*(4), 317–334.

Coutinho, M. J., & Oswald, D. P. (2005). State variation in gender disproportionality in special education: Findings and recommendations. *Remedial and Special Education, 26*(1), 7–15.

Creamer, J. (2020, September 15). Inequalities persist despite decline in poverty for all major race and Hispanic origin groups. *United States Census Bureau*. https://www.census.gov/library/stories/2020/09/poverty-rates-for-blacks-and-hispanics-reached-historic-lows-in-2019.html

Crenshaw, K., Ocen, P., & Nanda, J. (2015). *Black girls matter: Pushed out, over-policed and under-protected*. New York, NY: African American Policy Forum, Center for Intersectionality and Social Policy Studies.

Cui, J., & Natzke, L. (2020). Early Childhood Program Participation: 2019. First Look. NCES 2020-075. *National Center for Education Statistics*. http://nces.ed.gov/pubsearch/pubsinfo.asp?pubid=2020075

Cui, J., Natzke, L., & Grady, S. (2020). *Early childhood program participation: 2019*. National Center for Education Statistics, Institute of Education Sciences. https://files.eric.ed.gov/fulltext/ED607038.pdf

Curenton, S. M., Iruka, I. U., Humphries, M., Jensen, B., Durden, T., Rochester, S. E., Sims, J., Whittaker, J. V., & Kinzie, M. B. (2020). Validity for the assessing classroom sociocultural equity scale (ACSES) in early childhood classrooms. *Early Education and Development*, *31*(2), 269–288.

Cutler, A., & Gilkerson, L. (2002). *Unmet needs project: A research, coalition building, and policy initiative on the unmet needs of infants, toddlers, and families—Final report*. Accessed May 27, 2020. https://www.erikson.edu/wp-content/uploads/2017/10/unmetneedsreport1.pdf

Dancy, T. E. (2014). *The adultification of Black boys*. (K. J. Fasching-Varner, R. E. Reynolds, K. A. Albert, & L. L. Martin, Eds.). Sense.

Davis, A., Drazen, Y., Loomis, A., Padilla, C., & Cruden, G. (2020, February 5)). *A working framework for research-informed legislation prohibiting preschool expulsion and suspension*. Webinar presented to the Institute for Research on Povert. Recording available from https://www.irp.wisc.edu/resource/working-framework-for-research-informed-legislation-prohibiting-preschool-expulsion-suspension/

Davis, A. E., & Perry, D. F. (2016). *Pennsylvania Early Childhood Mental Health Consultation Project*. Center for Child and Human Development, Georgetown University, Washington, DC. https://www.iecmhc.org/wp-content/uploads/2020/12/PA_ECMHC_Report_Updated_executive-summary.pdf

Davis, A. E., Perry, D. F., & Rabinovitz, L. (2020). Expulsion prevention: Framework for the role of infant and early childhood mental health consultation in addressing implicit biases. *Infant Mental Health Journal*, *41*(3), 327–339.

Davis, A. E., Shivers, E. M., & Perry, D. F. (2018). Exploring culture, race, and ethnicity in early childhood mental health consultation: The role of the consultative alliance. *Perspectives on Early Childhood Psychology and Education*, *32*(2), 149–171.

de Heus, P., & Diekstra, R. F. W. (1999). Do teachers burn out more easily? A comparison of teachers with other social professions on work stress and burnout symptoms. In R. Vandenberghe & A. M. Huberman (Eds.), *Understanding and preventing teacher burnout*. Cambridge University Press.

Dee, T. (2005). A teacher like me: Does race, ethnicity or gender matter? *American Educational Association*, *95*(2), 158–165.

Downer, J. T., Goble, P., Myers, S. S., & Pianta, R. C. (2016). Teacher-child racial/ethnic match within pre-kindergarten classrooms and children's early school adjustment. *Early Child Research Quarterly*, *37*, 26–38.

Downer, J. T., & Myers, S. S. (2010). Application of a developmental/ecological model to school-family partnerships. In S. Christenson & A. L. Reschly (Eds.), *Handbook of school-family partnerships* (pp. 3–29). New York, NY: Routledge.

Dumas, M. J., & Nelson, J. D. (2016). (Re) Imagining Black boyhood: Toward a critical framework for educational research. *Harvard Educational Review, 86*(1), 27–47.

Durlak, J. A., Weissberg, R. P., Dymnicki, A. B., Taylor, R. D., & Schellinger, K. (2011). The impact of enhancing students' social and emotional learning: A meta-analysis of school-based universal interventions. *Child Development, 82*, 405–432.

Egger, H. L., & Angold, A. (2006). Common emotional and behavioral disorders in preschool children: presentation, nosology, and epidemiology. *The Journal of Child Psychology and Psychiatry, 47*(3–4), 313–337.

Esaki, N., & Larkin, H. (2013). Prevalence of adverse childhood experiences (ACEs) among child service providers. *Families in Society, 94*(1), 31–37.

Fadus, M. C., Ginsburg, K. R., Sobowale, K., Halliday-Boykins, C. A., Bryant, B. E., Gray, K. M., & Squeglia, L. M. (2020). Unconscious bias and the diagnosis of disruptive behavior disorders and ADHD in African American and Hispanic youth. *Academic Psychiatry, 44*(1), 95–102.

Ford, D. Y., & Russo, C. J. (2016). Historical and legal overview of special education overrepresentation: Access and equity denied. *Multiple Voices for Ethnically Diverse Exceptional Learners, 16*(1), 50–57.

Fox, L., Dunlap, G., Hemmeter, M. L., Joseph, G. E., & Strain, P. S. (2003). The Teaching Pyramid: A model for supporting social competence and preventing challenging behavior in young children. *Young Children, 58*(4), 48–52.

Friedman-Krauss, A. H., Raver, C. C., Morris, P. A., & Jones, S. M. (2014). The role of classroom-level child behavior problems in predicting preschoolteacher stress and classroom emotional climate. *Early Education and Development, 25*(4), 530–552.

Gershenson, S., Hart, C. M. D., Hyman, J., Lindsay, C., & Papageorge, N. W. (2018). *The long-run impacts of same-race teachers* (No. 25254). National Bureau of Economic Research.

Gibson, P. A., & Haight, W. (2013). Caregivers' moral narratives of their African American children's out-of-school suspensions: Implications for effective family-school collaborations. *Social Work, 58*(3), 263–272.

Gilliam, W. S. (2005). *Prekindergarteners left behind: Expulsion rates in state prekindergarten systems*. Yale University, New Haven, CT.

Gilliam, W. S. (2007). *Early childhood consultation partnership: Results of a random-controlled evaluation: Final report and executive summary*. Yale University, New Haven, CT.

Gilliam, W. S., Maupin, A. N., & Reyes, C. R. (2016). Early childhood mental health consultation: Results of a state-wide random-controlled evaluation. *Journal of the American Academy of Child & Adolescent Psychiatry, 55*(9), 754–761.

Gilliam, W. S., Maupin, A. N., Reyes, C. R., Accavitti, M., & Shic, F. (2016). Do early educators' implicit biases regarding sex and race relate to behavior expectations and recommendations of preschool expulsions and suspensions? *Yale University Child Study Center, 9*(28), 1–16.

Gilliam, W. S., & Reyes, C. R. (2018). Teacher decision factors that lead to preschool expulsion. *Infants and Young Children, 31*(2), 93–108.

Gilliam, W. S., & Shahar, G. (2006). Preschool and child care expulsion and suspension: Rates and predictors in one state. *Infants and Young Children, 19*(3), 228–245.

Glock, S., & Kleen, H. (2017). Gender and student misbehavior: Evidence from implicit and explicit measures. *Teaching and Teacher Education*, *67*, 93–103.

Goddard, R. D., Hoy, W. K., & Hoy, A. W. (2004). Collective efficacy beliefs: Theoretical developments, empirical evidence, and future directions. *Educational Researcher*, *33*(3), 3–13.

Goff, P. A., Jackson, M. C., Di Leone, B. A. L., Culotta, C. M., & DiTomasso, N. A. (2014). The essence of innocence: Consequences of dehumanizing black children. *Journal of Personality and Social Psychology*, *106*(4), 526–545.

Gordon, R. A., Sheridan, K., Bates, J., de Souza, S., & Pradzinski, A. (2020). Child care arrangements and gender: A national portrait of preschool-aged children. *Early Childhood Research Quarterly*, *53*, 40–49.

Gould, E., & Wilson, V. (2020, June 1). Black workers face two of the most lethal preexisting conditions for coronavirus—racism and economic inequality. *Economic Policy Institute*. https://www.epi.org/publication/black-workers-covid/

Gregory, A., Skiba, R. J., & Noguera, P. A. (2010). The achievement gap and the discipline gap: Two sides of the same coin? *Educational Researcher*, *39*(1), 59–68.

Gregory, A., & Weinstein, R. S. (2008). The discipline gap and African Americans: Defiance or cooperation in the high school classroom. *Journal of School Psychology*, *46*(4), 455–475.

Grossman-Kahn, S., Reyes C. R., Maupin A. N., & Gilliam, W. S. (2018, April 17). *Mapping Preschool expulsion legislation and policies*. Paper presented at the American Educational Research Association annual conference, New York.

Guarino, A. (2021). FAQ on the Child Care and Preschool Provisions in the Build Back Better Act. First Five Years Fund. https://www.ffyf.org/faq-on-the-child-care-and-preschool-provisions-in-the-build-back-better-act/

Hamre, B. K., & Pianta, R. C. (2001). Early teacher–child relationships and the trajectory of children's school outcomes through eighth grade. *Child Development*, *72*(2), 625–638.

Hauser-Cram, P., Sirin, S. R., & Stipek, D. (2003). When teachers' and parents' values differ: Teachers' ratings of academic competence in children from low-income families. *Journal of Educational Psychology*, *95*(4), 813–820.

Heckman, J. J. (2006). Skill formation and the economics of investing in disadvantaged children. *Science 2*, *312*, 1900–1902.

Heckman, J. J., & Karapakula, G. (2019). *Intergenerational and intragenerational externalities of the Perry Preschool Project* (No. w25889). National Bureau of Economic Research.

Hemmeter, M. L., Fox, L., Jack, S., & Broyles, L. (2007). A program-wide model of positive behavior support in early childhood settings. *Journal of Early Intervention*, *29*(4), 337–355.

Hemmeter, M. L., Snyder, P. A., & Fox, L., Algina, J. (2016). Evaluating the implementation of the Pyramid Model for promoting social-emotional competence in early childhood classrooms. *Topics in Early Childhood Special Education*, *36*(3), 133–146.

Hemmeter, M. L., Snyder, P., & Fox, L. (2018). Using the Teaching Pyramid Observation Tool (TPOT) to support implementation of social–emotional teaching practices. *School Mental Health*, *10*(3), 202–213.

Henneman, T. K. (2014). *Preschool expulsions: Parental experiences of Black boys who were pushed out or left behind*. Mills College.

Herman, K. C., & Reinke, W. M. (2017). Improving teacher perceptions of parent involvement patterns: Findings from a group randomized trial. *School Psychology Quarterly, 32*(1), 89–104.

Hobbs, N. (1982). *The troubled and troubling child: Reeducation in mental health, education, and human services programs for children and youth*. Jossey-Bass.

Hoffman, K. M., Trawalter, S., Axt, J. R., & Oliver, M. N. (2016). Racial bias in pain assessment and treatment recommendations, and false beliefs about biological differences between blacks and whites. *Proceedings of the National Academy of Sciences, 113*(16), 4296–4301.

Hooper, A., & Schweiker, C. (2012). Prevalence and predictors of expulsion in home-based child care settings. *Infant Mental Health Journal, 41*(3), 411–425.

Hoover, S. D., Kubicek, L. F., Rosenberg, C. R., Zundel, C., & Rosenberg, S. A. (2012). Influence of behavioral concerns and early childhood expulsions on the development of early childhood mental health consultation in Colorado. *Infant Mental Health Journal, 33*(3), 246–255.

Hoover, S., & Stainback-Tracy, K. (2007). *Mental health consultation in early care and education: A resource and sustainability toolkit for providers*. Denver: JFK Partners, University of Colorado, Denver.

Howard, A. R. H., Parris, S., Hall, J. S., Call, C. D., Razuri, E. B., Purvis, K. B., & Cross, D. R. (2015). An examination of the relationships between professional quality of life, adverse childhood experiences, resilience, and work environment in a sample of human service providers. *Children and Youth Services Review, 57*, 141–148.

Howard, K. M., & Lipinoga, S. (2010). Closing down openings: Pretextuality and misunderstanding in parent–teacher conferences with Mexican immigrant families. *Language and Communication, 30*(1), 33–47.

Hubel, G. S., Davies, F., Goodrum, N. M., Schmarder, K. M., Schnake, K., & Moreland, A. D. (2020). Adverse childhood experiences among early care and education teachers: Prevalence and associations with observed quality of classroom social and emotional climate. *Children and Youth Services Review, 111*, 104877.

Hunt, T. K. A., Slack, K. S., & Berger, L. M. (2017). Adverse childhood experiences and behavioral problems in middle childhood. *Child Abuse & Neglect, 67*, 391–402.

Hwang, N. (2018). Suspensions and achievement: Varying links by type, frequency, and subgroup. *Educational Researcher, 47*(6), 363–374.

Dancy, T. E. (2014). (Un)doing hegemony in education: Disrupting school-to-prison pipelines for black males. *Equity & Excellence in Education, 47*, 476–493.

Erikson Institute. (2019). *Illinois Risk and Reach Report*. Erikson Institute, Chicago, IL.

Iruka, I. U., Burchinal, M., & Cai, K. (2010). Long-term effect of early relationships for African American children's academic and social development: An examination from kindergarten to fifth grade. *Journal of Black Psychology, 36*(2), 144–171.

Iruka, I., Curenton, S. M., Durden, T. R., & Escayg, K. A. (2020). *Don't look away: Embracing anti-bias classrooms*. Gryphon House.

Ispa-Landa S. (2018). Persistently harsh punishments amid efforts to reform: Using tools from social psychology to counteract racial bias in school disciplinary decisions. *Educational Researcher, 47*(6), 384–390.

Jargowsky, P. (2015, August 7). Architecture of segregation: Civil unrest, the concentration of poverty, and public policy. *The Century Foundation and Center for Urban Research and Education, Rutgers-Camden*. Retrieved from: http://apps. tcf. org/architecture-of-segregation

Jennings, P. A. (2011). Promoting teachers' social and emotional competencies to support performance and reduce burnout. In A. Cohan & A. Honigsfeld (Eds.), *Breaking the mold of preservice and inservice teacher education* (pp. 133–143). Rowman & Littlefield.

Jennings, P. A., & Greenberg, M. T. (2009). The prosocial classroom: Teacher social and emotional competence in relation to student and classroom outcomes. *Review of Educational Research, 79*(1), 491–525.

Jerome, E. M., Hamre, B. K., & Pianta, R. C. (2009). Teacher–child relationships from kindergarten to sixth grade: Early childhood predictors of teacher-perceived conflict and closeness. *Social Development, 18*, 915–945.

Johnson, S., Cooper, C., Cartwright, S., Donald, I., Taylor, P., & Millet, C. (2005). The experience of work-related stress across occupations. *Journal of Managerial Psychology, 20*(2), 178–187.

Johnson, T. J., Hickey, R. W., Switzer, G. E., Miller, E., Winger, D. G., Nguyen, M., . . . & Hausmann, L. R. (2016). The impact of cognitive stressors in the emergency department on physician implicit racial bias. *Academic Emergency Medicine, 23*(3), 297–305.

Jones, D. E., Greenberg, M., & Crowley, M. (2015). Early social-emotional functioning and public health: The relationship between kindergarten social competence and future wellness. *American Journal of Public Health, 105*(11), 2283–2290.

Kahneman, D. (2011). *Thinking, fast and slow*. Macmillan.

Krezmien, M. P., Leone, P. E., & Achilles, G. M. (2006). Suspension, race, and disability: Analysis of statewide practices and reporting. *Journal of Emotional and Behavioral Disorders, 14*(4), 217–226. https://doi.org/10.1177/10634266060140040501

Lahey, B. B., Van Hulle, C. A., D'Onofrio, B. M., Rogers, J. L., & Waldman, I. D. (2008). Is parental knowledge of their adolescent offspring's whereabouts and peer associations spuriously associated with offspring delinquency? *Journal of Abnormal Child Psychology, 36*, 807–823.

Lang, S. N., Schoppe-Sullivan, S. J., & Jeon, L. (2017). Examining a self-report measure of parent–teacher cocaring relationships and associations with parental involvement. *Early Education and Development, 28*(1), 96–114.

Lawson, M. A. (2003). School-family relations in context: Parent and teacher perceptions of parent involvement. *Urban Education, 38*(1), 77–133.

Lee, T., Cornell, D., Gregory, A., & Fan, X. (2011). High suspension schools and dropout rates for Black and White students. *Education and Treatment of Children, 34*(2), 167–192.

Lewis, A. E., & Diamond, J. B. (2015). *Despite the best intentions: How racial inequality thrives in good schools*. Oxford University Press.

Lewis, M. M., Garces, L. M., & Frankenberg, E. (2019). A comprehensive and practical approach to policy guidance: The Office for Civil Rights' role in education during the Obama administration. *Educational Researcher, 48*(1), 51–60.

Lipscomb, S. T., Hatfield, B., Lewis, H., Goka-Dubose, E., & Abshire, C. (2021). Adverse childhood experiences and children's development in early care and education programs. *Journal of Applied Developmental Psychology, 72*, 101218.

Losen, D. J. (2015). *Closing the school discipline gap: Equitable remedies for excessive exclusion*. Teachers College Press.

Losen, D. J., Hodson, C. L., Keith, M. A., II, Morrison, K., & Belway, S. (2015, February 23). *Are we closing the school discipline gap?* The Center for Civil Rights Remedies, University of California, Los Angeles.

Lott, B. (2001). Low-income parents and the public schools. *Journal of Social Issues, 57*(2), 247–259.

Main, C., Yarbrough, K. W., & Patten, B. (2018). *Voices from the front lines of early learning: 2017 Illinois Early Childhood Workforce Survey Report.* University of Illinois at Chicago, College of Education.

Malik, R. (2017). New data reveal 250 preschoolers are suspended or expelled every day. Retrieved from Center for American Progress website: https://www.americanprogress.org/issues/early-childhood/news/2017/11/06/442280/new-data-reveal-250-preschoolers-suspended-expelled-every-day

Martin, K. A., Bosk, E., & Bailey, D. (2018). Teachers' perceptions of child care and preschool expulsion. *Children and Society, 32*(2), 87–97.

Mavropoulou, S., & Padeliadu, S. (2002). Teachers' causal attributions for behaviour problems in relation to perceptions of control. *Educational Psychology, 22*(2), 191–202.

McCann, C., Smith, S., Nguyen, U., & Granja, M. R. (2021). States' Growing Commitment to Preventing Young Children's Expulsion from Early Care and Education Programs: Results of a 50-State Policy Survey. *National Center for Children in Poverty.* https://www.nccp.org/publication/states-growing-commitment-to-preventing-young-childrens-expulsion-from-early-care-and-education-programs/

McClowry, S. G., Rodriguez, E. T., Tamis-LeMonda, C. S., Spellmann, M. E., Carlson, A., & Snow, D. L. (2013). Teacher/student interactions and classroom behavior: The role of student temperament and gender. *Journal of Research in Childhood Education, 27*(3), 283–301.

Meek, S., Smith, L., Allen, R., Catherine, E., Edyburn, K., Williams, C., Fabes, R., McIntosh, K., Garcia, E., Takanishi, R., & Gordon, L. (2020). Start with equity: From the early years to the early grades. Children's Equity Project and Bipartisan Policy Center. Available from https://childandfamilysuccess.asu.edu/cep/start-with-equity

Morgan, P. L., Farkas, G., Cook, M., Strassfeld, N. M., Hillemeier, M. M., Pun, W. H., & Schussler, D. L. (2017). Are Black children disproportionately overrepresented in special education? A best-evidence synthesis. *Exceptional Children, 83*(2), 181–198.

Morsy, L., & Rothstein, R. (2019, May 1). Toxic stress and children's outcomes. *Economic Policy Institute.* https://www.epi.org/publication/toxic-stress-and-childrens-outcomes-african-american-children-growing-up-poor-are-at-greater-risk-of-disrupted-physiological-functioning-and-depressed-academic-achievement/

Mundt, K., Gregory, A., Melzi, G., & McWayne, C. M. (2015). The influence of ethnic match on Latino school-based family engagement. *Hispanic Journal of Behavioral Sciences, 37*(2), 170–185.

National Academies of Sciences, Engineering, and Medicine. (2015). *Mental Disorders and Disabilities Among Low-Income Children.* Washington, DC: The National Academies Press. https://doi.org/10.17226/21780

National Academies of Sciences, Engineering, and Medicine. [NASEM]. (2019). *Vibrant and healthy kids: Aligning science, practice, and policy to advance health equity.* National Academies Press.

National Research Council. (2015). *Transforming the workforce for children birth through age 8: A unifying foundation.* National Academies Press (US).

National Research Council (US) and Institute of Medicine (US) Committee on Integrating the Science of Early Childhood Development. (2000). *From neurons to neighborhoods: The science of early childhood development* (J. P. Shonkoff & D. A. Phillips, Eds.). National Academies Press (US).

National Scientific Council on the Developing Child. (2014). Excessive stress disrupts the architecture of the developing brain. *Journal of Children's Services, 9*(2), 143–153.

Newcomb, M. D., Abbott, R. D., Catalano, R. F., Hawkins, J. D., Battin-Pearson, S., & Hill, K. (2002). Mediational and deviance theories of late high school failure: Process roles of structural strains, academic competence, and general versus specific problem behavior. *Journal of Counseling Psychology, 49*(2), 172–186.

Noltemeyer, A. L., Ward, R. M., & McLoughlin, C. (2015). Relationship between school suspension and student outcomes: A meta-analysis. *School Psychology Review, 44*(2), 224–240. https://doi.org/10.17105/spr-14-0008.1

Okonofua, J. A., & Eberhardt, J. L. (2015). Two strikes: Race and the disciplining of young students. *Psychological Science, 26*(5), 617–624.

Okonofua, J. A., Paunesku, D., & Walton, G. M. (2016). Brief intervention to encourage empathic discipline cuts suspension rates in half among adolescents. *Proceedings of the National Academy of Sciences, 113*(19), 5221–5226.

Perry, D. F., Dunne, M. C., McFadden, L., & Campbell, D. (2008). Reducing the risk for preschool expulsion: Mental health consultation for young children with challenging behaviors. *Journal of Child and Family Studies, 17*, 44–54.

Petras, H., Masyn, K. E., Buckley, J. A., Ialongo, N. S., & Kellam, S. (2011). Who is most at risk for school removal? A multilevel discrete-time survival analysis of individual-and context-level influences. *Journal of Educational Psychology, 103*(1), 223–237.

Phillips, D., Austin, L., & Whitebook, M. (2016). The early care and education workforce. *The Future of Children, 26*(2), 139–158.

Public Act 100-0105. (2018). https://www.ilga.gov/legislation/publicacts/fulltext.asp?Name=100-0105 Illinois General Assembly

Quesenberry, A. C., Hemmeter, M. L., Ostrosky, M. M., & Hamann, K. (2014). Child care teachers' perspectives on including children with challenging behavior in child care settings. *Infants and, 27*(3), 241–258.

Raffeaele Mendez, & Knoff, H. M. (2003). Who gets suspended from school and why: A demographic analysis of schools and disciplinary infractions in a large school district. *Education and Treatment of Children, 26*(1), 30–51.

Ratcliff, N., & Hunt, G. (2009). Building teacher-family partnerships: The role of teacher preparation programs. *Education, 129*(3), 495–505.

Riddle, T., & Sinclair, S. (2019). Racial disparities in school-based disciplinary actions are associated with county-level rates of racial bias. *Proceedings of the National Academy of Sciences, 116*(17), 8255–8260.

Roger D., & Hudson, C. (1995). The role of emotion control and emotional rumination in stress management training. *International Journal of Stress Management, 2*, 119–132.

Rose, S. M., Xie, D., & Stineman, M. (2014). Adverse childhood experiences and disability in U.S. Adults. *PM&R, 6*(8), 670–680.

Rudman, L. A. (2004). Social justice in our minds, homes, and society: The nature, causes, and consequences of implicit bias. *Social Justice Research, 17*, 129–142.

Ryan, B., Adams, G., Gullotta, T., Weissberg, R., & Hampton, R. (1995). *The family-school connection: Theory, research, and practice*. Sage.

Schonert-Reichl, K. A., Hanson-Peterson, J. L., & Hymel, S. (2015). SEL and pre-service teacher education. In J. A. Durlak, C. E. Domitrovich, R. P. Weissberg, & T. P. Gullotta (Eds.), *Handbook of social and emotional learning: Research and practice* (pp. 406–421). The Guilford Press.

Schweinhart, L. J. (1993). *Significant benefits: The High/Scope Perry Preschool Study through age 27. Monographs of the High/Scope Educational Research Foundation, no. Ten*. High/Scope Educational Research Foundation.

Serpell, Z. N., & Mashburn, A. J. (2012). Family–school connectedness and children's early social development. *Social Development*, *21*(1), 21–46.

Shaw, D. S., Bell, R. Q., & Gilliom, M. (2000). A truly early starter model of antisocial behavior revisited. *Clinical Child and Family Psychology Review*, *33*(3), 155–172.

Sheffield, D., Dobbie, D., & Carroll, D. (1994). Stress, social support, and psychological and physical well-being in secondary school teachers. *Work and Stress*, *8*, 235–243.

Shelov, S. P., Altmann, T. R., & Hannemann, R. E. (2014). *Caring for your baby and young child, birth to age 5* (American Academy of Pediatrics, Ed.; 6th ed.). Bantam Books.

Shivers, E. M., Gal, D., & Meaney, C. (2019). *Evaluation of Alameda County Behavioral Health Early Childhood Mental Health Consultation Standards of Practice Training and Technical Assistance Pilot*. Alameda County Behavior Health and Indigo Cultural Center.

Shonkoff, J. P., Garner, A. S., Siegel, B. S., Dobbins, M. I., Earls, M. F., McGuinn, L., Pascoe, J., Wood, D. L., Committee on Psychosocial Aspects of Child and Family Health and Committee on Early Childhood, Adoption, and Dependent Care. (2012). The lifelong effects of early childhood adversity and toxic stress. *Pediatrics*, *129*(1), e232–e246.

Shonkoff, J. P., Phillips, D. A., & National Research Council. (2000). The developing brain. In *From neurons to neighborhoods: The science of early childhood development*. National Academies Press (US).

Silver, H. C., & Zinsser, K. M. (2020). The interplay among early childhood teachers' social and emotional well-being, mental health consultation, and preschool expulsion. *Early Education and Development*, *31*(7), 1133–1150.

Silver, H. C., Zinsser, K. M., Zulauf-McCurdy, C. A., Lowe-Fotos, A., Estlund, M., & Orr, L. (2021). Transforming early childhood discipline policy through collaborative research and evaluation. *Translational Issues in Psychological Science*. *7*(1), 21–34. https://doi.org/10.1037/tps0000279

Skiba, R., Peterson, R., & Williams, T. (1997). Office referrals and suspension: Disciplinary intervention in middle schools. *Education and Treatment of Children*, *20*(3), 295–315.

Skiba, R. J., Horner, R. H., Chung, C.-G., Rausch, M. K., May, S. L., & Tobin, T. (2011). Race is not neutral: A national investigation of African American and Latino disproportionality in school discipline. *School Psychology Review*, *40*(1), 85–107.

Skiba, R. J., Michael, R. S., Nardo, A. C., & Peterson, R. L. (2002). The color of discipline: Sources of racial and gender disproportionality in school punishment. *The Urban Review*, *34*, 317–342.

Skiba, R., & Rausch, M. K. (2004, July 9). The relationship between achievement, discipline, and race: An analysis of factors predicting ISTEP scores. *Center for Evaluation and Education Policy*. Children Left Behind Policy Briefs, Supplementary Analysis 2-D. https://files.eric.ed.gov/fulltext/ED488899.pdf

Smith, S., & McCann, C. (2020). *BUILD/NCCP expulsion survey*. [Unpublished Work]. National Center for Children in Poverty, Bank Street Graduate School of Education, New York.

Smith, T. E., & Sheridan, S. M. (2019). The effects of teacher training on teachers' family-engagement practices, attitudes, and knowledge: A meta-analysis. *Journal of Educational and Psychological Consultation*, *29*(2), 128–157.

Smith, T. E., Sheridan, S. M., Kim, E. M., Park, S., & Beretvas, S. N. (2020). The effects of family-school partnership interventions on academic and social-emotional functioning: A meta-analysis exploring what works for whom. *Educational Psychology Review, 32*(2), 511–544.

Stebnicki, M. A. (2008). *Empathy fatigue: Healing the mind, body, and spirit of professional counselors*. Springer.

Stinchcomb, J. B., Bazemore, G., & Riestenberg, N. (2006). Beyond zero tolerance: Restoring justice in secondary schools. *Youth Violence and Juvenile Justice, 4*(2), 123–147.

Tatum, B. D. (2003). *Why are all the Black kids sitting together in the cafeteria? And other conversations about race*. Basic Books.

Tellenback, S., Brenner, S.-O., & Horst Löfgren. (1983). Teacher stress: Exploratory model building. *Journal of Occupational Psychology, 56*(1), 19–33.

Tenenbaum, H. R., & Ruck, M. D. (2007). Are teachers' expectations different for racial minority than for European American students? A meta-analysis. *Journal of Educational Psychology, 99*(2), 253–273.

Thomas, D., & Fry, R. (2020, November 30). Prior to COVID-19, child poverty rates had reached record lows in U.S. *Pew Research Center*. https://www.pewresearch.org/fact-tank/2020/11/30/prior-to-covid-19-child-poverty-rates-had-reached-record-lows-in-u-s/

Thomason, A. C., & La Paro, K. M. (2013). Teachers' commitment to the field and teacher–child interactions in center-based child care for toddlers and three-year-olds. *Early Childhood Education Journal, 41*, 227–234.

Torres, L. M. (2019). *Predictors of parent-teacher relationship quality in Head Start classrooms*. Thesis, University of Illinois at Chicago. https://doi.org/10.25417/uic.12480896.v1

Townsend, L., Flisher, A. J., & King, G. (2007). A systematic review of the relationship between high school dropout and substance use. *Clinical Child and Family Psychology Review, 10*(4), 295–317.

Tseng, V., & Seidman, E. (2007). A systems framework for understanding social settings. *American Journal of Community Psychology, 39*(3–4), 217–228.

Upshur, C., Wenz-Gross, M., & Reed, G. (2009). A pilot study of early childhood mental health consultation for children with behavioral problems in preschool. *Early Childhood Research Quarterly, 24*(2), 29–45.

U.S. Department of Education Office for Civil Rights. (2014 March 21). *Data snapshot: School discipline, issue brief no. 1*. U.S. Department of Education.

U.S. Department of Health & Human Services (2016). *Head Start Program Performance Standards (HSPPS) final rule ACF-PI-HS-16-04*. Head Start Early Childhood Learning & Knowledge Center https://eclkc.ohs.acf.hhs.gov/policy/pi/acf-pi-hs-16-04

U.S. Department of Health and Human Services (DHHS) & U.S. Department of Education (DOE) (2014). *Policy statement on expulsion and suspension policies in early childhood settings*. U.S. Department of Health and Human Services & U.S. Department of Education https://www2.ed.gov/policy/gen/guid/school-discipline/policy-statement-ece-expulsions-suspensions.pdf

Vincent, C. G., Swain-Bradway, J., Tobin, T. J., & May, S. (2011). Disciplinary referrals for culturally and linguistically diverse students with and without disabilities: Patterns resulting from school-wide positive behavior support. *Exceptionality, 19*(3), 175–190.

Vinh, M., Strain, P., Davidson, S., & Smith, B. J. (2016). One state's systems change efforts to reduce child care expulsion: Taking the Pyramid Model to scale. *Topics in Early Childhood Special Education*, *36*(3), 159–164.

Waldfogel, J., Garfinkel, I., & Kelly, B. (2007). Welfare and the Cost of Public Assistance. In C. R. Belfield & H. M. Levin (Eds.), *The price we pay: The social and economic costs to the nation of inadequate education* (pp. 16–176). Brookings Institution Press.

Wallace, J. M., Jr., Goodkind, S., Wallace, C. M., & Bachman, J. G. (2008). Racial, ethnic, and gender differences in school discipline among US high school students: 1991–2005. *The Negro Educational Review*, *59*(1-2), 47–62.

Watts, T. W., Gandhi, J., Ibrahim, D. A., & Masucci, R. C. (2018). The Chicago School Readiness Project: Examining the long-term impacts of an early childhood intervention. *PLoS ONE*, *13*(7), 1–25. https://doi.org/10.1371/journal.pone.0200144

Welch, K., & Payne, A. A. (2010). Racial threat and punitive school discipline. *Social Problems*, *57*(1), 25–48.

Welsh, R. O., & Little, S. (2018). The school discipline dilemma: A comprehensive review of disparities and alternative approaches. *Review of Educational Research*, *88*(5), 752–794.

Wentzel, K. R. (2002). Are effective teachers like good parents? Teaching styles and student adjustment in early adolescence. *Child Development*, *73*(1), 287–301.

Whitaker, R. C., Becker, B. D., Herman, A. N., & Goose, R. A. (2013). The physical and mental health of Head Start staff: The Pennsylvania Head Start staff wellness survey, 2012. *Preventing Chronic Disease*, *10*, 130–170. http://dx.doi.org/10.5888/pcd10.130171

Winn, D. M., Iruka, I. U., Harradine, C., Buansi, A., McKinney, M., & Stevenson, H. (2012). *Providing opportunities to spite the obstacles: Countering the adverse conditions that undermine the success of African American boys*. Insight, Washington, DC: Grantmakers for Children Youth and Families Press.

Yoshikawa, H., & Zigler, E. (2000). Mental health in Head Start: New directions for the twenty-first century. *Early Education and Development*, *11*(3), 247–264.

Yosso, T. J. (2005). Whose culture has capital? A critical race theory discussion of community cultural wealth. *Race Ethnicity and Education*, *8*(1), 69–91.

Zeng, S., Pereira, B., Larson, A., Corr, C. P., O'Grady, C., & Stone-MacDonald, A. (2020). Preschool suspension and expulsion for young children with disabilities. *Exceptional Children*, *87*(2), 199–216. https://doi.org/10.1177/0014402920949832

Zeng, S., Corr, C. P., O'Grady, C., & Guan, Y. (2019). Adverse childhood experiences and preschool suspension expulsion: A population study. *Child Abuse & Neglect*, *97*, 104–149.

Zinsser, K. M., Bailey, C. S., Curby, T. W., Susanne A. D., & Bassett, H. H. (2013). Exploring the predictable classroom: Preschool teacher stress, emotional supportiveness, and students' social-emotional behavior in private and Head Start classrooms. *NHSA Dialog*, *16*(2), 90–108.

Zinsser, K., Silver, H. C., Jackson, V., & Shenberger, E. (2022). A systematic review of early childhood exclusionary discipline. *Review of Educational Research*. https://doi.org/10.3102/00346543211070047

Zinsser, K. M., Zulauf, C. A., Nair Das, V., & Silver, H. C. (2019). Utilizing social-emotional learning supports to address teacher stress and preschool expulsion. *Journal of Applied Developmental Psychology*, *61*, 33–42.

Zulauf-McCurdy, C. A., & Zinsser, K. M. (2021). How teachers' perceptions of the parent–teacher relationship affect children's risk for early childhood expulsion. *Psychology in the Schools*, *58*(1), 69–88.

Zulauf, C. A., & Zinsser, K. M. (2019). Forestalling preschool expulsion: A mixed-method exploration of the potential protective role of teachers' perceptions of parents. *American Educational Research Journal*, *56*(6), 2189–2022. https://doi.org/10.3102/0002831219838236

Index

For the benefit of digital users, indexed terms that span two pages (e.g., 52–53) may, on occasion, appear on only one of those pages.

Figures and notes are indicated by *f* and n following the page number